"We are living at a time of cultural shift. The postmodern mindset is gradually replacing the modern worldview. How can we communicate the gospel to a culture in transition? Do we need to rethink evangelism to reach our generation? In *Evangelism Outside the Box* Rick Richardson tackles these questions and comes up with some challenging answers."
NICKY GUMBEL, *chaplain, Alpha Course*

"Affirming that winning people to Jesus Christ is '100 percent God, 100 percent us,' Rick Richardson shakes off the dust of misconceptions and assumptions about today's seekers, revealing God's handprints on our own culture—a culture full of opportunities, if we'll only see them and grasp them."
LUIS PALAU, *evangelist, Luis Palau Evangelistic Association*

"If the contemporary church is going to reach this postmodern generation it will have to embrace new methods of evangelism. Rick Richardson's book is an extremely useful guide for this challenging task."
LYLE W. DORSETT, *professor of evangelism and spiritual formation, Wheaton College and Graduate School*

"Rick Richardson's book is disturbing on two levels: first, he refuses to let believers off the hook regarding lost persons in a lost culture. He dares to tell us to transform the culture and not condemn it. Second, he tells us 'old' evangelism ways won't work and suggests a new apologetic—just when the old ways were becoming comfortable to me. Disturbing—disturbing—disturbing. Thank God for those who disturb me!"
LON ALLISON, *director, Billy Graham Center, Wheaton College*

"Is witnessing for you something like hitting a handball into a sand dune? Lots of effort, little response? Have you found that the old answers, the 'proven' methods, just don't seem to work? Then read *Evangelism Outside the Box*. Rick Richardson listens to our culture with sensitive ears, asks probing questions, points to fresh approaches. I believe that his book, like Paul Little's *How to Give Away Your Faith* and Cliffe Knechtle's *Give Me An Answer*, will help us to connect with this seeking generation. I plan to recommend it widely."
LEIGHTON FORD, *president, Leighton Ford Ministries*

Evangelism

OUTSIDE THE BOX

New Ways
to Help
People
Experience
the Good
News

Rick Richardson

InterVarsity Press
Downers Grove, Illinois

InterVarsity Press
P.O. Box 1400, Downers Grove, IL 60515-1426
World Wide Web: www.ivpress.com
E-mail: mail@ivpress.com

InterVarsity Press® is the book-publishing division of InterVarsity Christian Fellowship/USA®, a student movement active on campus at hundreds of universities, colleges and schools of nursing in the United States of America, and a member movement of the International Fellowship of Evangelical Students. For information about local and regional activities, write Public Relations Dept., InterVarsity Christian Fellowship/USA, 6400 Schroeder Rd., P.O. Box 7895, Madison, WI 53707-7895.

Cover photograph: Michael Goss

ISBN 0-8308-2276-3

Printed in the United States of America ∞

Library of Congress Cataloging-in-Publication Data

Richardson, Rick, 1955-
   Evangelism outside the box : new ways to help people experience the Good News /
   Rick Richardson.
     p.   cm.
   Includes bibliographical references.
   ISBN 0-8308-2276-3 (pbk. : alk. paper)
    1. Evangelistic work.
   BV3790 .R533 2000
   269'.2—dc21

                           00-061365

18	17	16	15	14	13	12	11	10	9	8	7	6	5	4	3	2
14	13	12	11	10	09	08	07	06	05	04	03	02	01			

This book is dedicated to my wife, MaryKay,
who keeps me rooted in reality with both feet
(or at least one of them) on the ground
so that I can soar when the time
and the winds are right.
I love her dearly and appreciate her
warm-hearted encouragement of who I am
and the calling I have as an evangelist.
Thank you, dear heart!

CONTENTS

Acknowledgments

Many people made investments in my life that have made this book possible. I want to thank some of them here:

Peter Cha for being a friend, a prayer partner and my most helpful reviewer. He gently but insistently pushed me out of my mental boxes, many of which I hadn't even recognized.

Ray Bakke for bringing the Scriptures together with the world in ways that blew open the boxes I had built around both.

Bill Leslie for living all his life outside the box. He served and nurtured everyone around him who tried to do the same, and his memory still lingers almost daily.

Bill Hybels for reminding us all that lost people really do matter to God. He as much as anyone helped to open my eyes to see Jesus' heart, initiating my own evangelism revolution.

Mark Mittelberg for helping me to become more contagious and for encouraging me and InterVarsity Christian Fellowship in our evangelism revolution. He has not just coined phrases, he has lived them, and he has helped me to do the same.

Becky Pippert for helping me out of the saltshaker when I was in college years ago. Many of my stories come out of early attempts to meet the challenges in her book. Now that I know her, I am doubly inspired.

Jim Lundgren and Sandy Beelen, my supervisors, for helping me stay healthy enough as a human being to function as an author. Both have encouraged me in ways too numerous to mention.

Steve Hayner, president of InterVarsity Christian Fellowship, for sharpening my thinking, encouraging my ministry and telling me to "go for it" with this book before almost anyone else believed in the project.

Andy Le Peau, my editor, for helping me find my voice and express my ideas in ways that are authentic to who I am. He has been a delight to work with even as he has "corrected, rebuked, encouraged and trained" me in the ways of writing—a great gift.

Kara Brady, manager of my neighborhood Einstein Bagels, for letting me sip my coffee and eat my cinnamon sugar bagel for hours on end while writing the book.

My parents for illustrating with their lives what it means to have a vision and sense of responsibility for making a contribution to the greater good. (Thanks, Mom and Dad!)

Lee Strobel for trusting that pre-Christians still want to think. (He's right!)

Lon Allison for fanning into flame our mutual longing to keep evangelism and prayer inseparably intertwined.

My coconspirators past and present—Terry Erickson, Mark Slaughter, Mark Ashton, Mack Stiles, Phyllis Le Peau, Chris Swiney, Jenny Vaughan, John Teter, Peter Horton, Dick Ryan, Ruth Goring, Jan Martinet, Stewart Ruch, Kelly Larsen, Mike Hernberg, Geri Rodman, Jimmy Long (and the Emerging Culture Task Force), Paul and Marie Little, Pete Hammond, Rich Vroon and many others—for their efforts in the evangelism revolution at InterVarsity.

My brothers, Mike and Chris, for being so fun to flyfish with. They probably have no sense of how many of my ideas—keepers or not—were spawned while out on the streams with them.

And Chris, Steve and Colby, my three boys, whom I love dearly, for waiting so patiently for me to write the science fiction book.

Introduction

When I was six years old, I got an unforgettable picture of God's heart. My dad was in the military, stationed in North Carolina. Across from our family's home lived a family also in the military. We had three boys. They had three girls. Each Friday in warm weather our moms drove the six kids an hour to the beach, where we spent the day building sand castles and wading in the waves. Then we would pile back into a big, ugly green station wagon and return home.

On one of our trips back home, with us in the middle of the fifteenth verse of the song about Noah's "arky, arky" and the animals that came in by "twosies, twosies," Allison, the youngest girl, asked where Chris was. Chris was my youngest brother, three years old. He was a trickster, so we thought he must be hiding somewhere in the car. We looked under the beach blankets. We looked in the tire well. We searched the back of the car. No Chris. He must still be at the beach.

"Mom, Chris isn't here," I reported.

"Wha-a-a-a-t?" her mother responded. At that moment I began the ride of my life! Cheryl's mother hit the brake with magnum force. She spun that big, ugly green station wagon in a 180-degree turn, tires screeching. Then she put the pedal to the metal. What had been a thirty-minute trip from the beach took us fifteen minutes going back. I think we hit a hundred miles per hour, and we only stayed that low because it was an old car and just couldn't go any faster.

At the beach we piled out and ran back through the archway and onto the sand. We ran from guard station to guard station. At the last one, my mother saw Chris and Chris saw my mother. They called out to each other. They ran toward each other. And then it was like a scene from a movie. My mom caught Chris in her arms and twirled him, hugging him, laughing and crying all at the same time.

Chris was lost. My mother braved the curves of North Carolina roads and (it felt like) risked all our lives to find him. But that passionate mother-love for her lost child is only a glimmer of the passion of God for those who are lost and don't know Jesus. He wants to turn the big, ugly green station wagon (maybe an appropriate analogy for our church or ministry!) around and race to wherever these lost and hurting people can be found. But he's letting us drive. We are at the steering wheel of the green station wagon. If we are happy with who is already in the car and who is not, we can continue on home singing our fun travel songs.

God is looking for station wagon drivers who will collaborate with him to reach the lost and to fulfill the Great Commission. He 's looking for people who want to be like Jesus in Luke 15.

Getting Ready to Celebrate

In Luke 15, Jesus answers his critics by revealing his priorities. The religious people don't think he should be hanging out with all these "sinners," all these lost people. Jesus is a religious teacher, they say. He should hang out with religious people. All these broken, lost, sick, sinful people will corrupt him.

Jesus makes a captivating reply. He tells some great stories. He talks about normal stuff: a sheep, a coin, a son. Everyday life stuff. And he weaves several common themes through each story. Something or someone has been lost. A sheep. A coin. A son. What is lost is very valuable to the person who lost it. That person engages in an all-out search. The shepherd hikes the hills far and wide, searching everywhere for his lost sheep. The woman turns her house upside down searching for her lost coin. She creates a major cleanup job for herself, because her desire for order is minuscule in comparison to her longing for what has been lost. In the case of the son, who chose to go to the far country, the father knows a search will be futile until the son wants to return. But he engages in active, anxious, daily waiting and watching, so as not to miss the opportunity to respond to any change in heart. In all three stories, when what was lost gets found, there is an all-out, raucous, rowdy, over-the-top celebration. Party on! The lost has been found! The shepherd, the woman, the father cannot keep their joy to themselves. Everybody is invited to share in the party, in some cases whether they want to or not.

Religious people tend to create programs and ministries that meet the needs of other religious people. Jesus knew that. He chose a different way. At the cost of his life, he chose to find the lost, to heal the sick, to cure the sinner. He wants his church to fulfill his ministry and embrace his priority.

Lost people matter to God. God is on an all-out search to find them. He wants partners. He wants partners in sacrifice. We sacrifice order. We sacrifice neatness. We sacrifice control. We sacrifice the comfort that comes with only meeting the needs of people like ourselves. We sacrifice the tranquillity of those who close their eyes to the eternal needs of others.

But the payback far outweighs the pain. For the joy set before us, we endure the pain of sacrifice. We are invited to an everlasting party, where every little step we took to reach the lost, every little sacrifice we made, will pale in comparison to the weight of glory and the eternal jubilation that will mark the lives of all who helped even one sinner come home.

I believe that about God and his heart. If you're reading this book, I'll bet you believe that too.

How Can We Refuel?

So why is it a struggle to maintain our passion for people outside God's family? Why do we lose our commitment and energy and effectiveness in evangelism so easily? Maybe you can relate to the following story if you've ever been involved in a church or ministry that tried to sponsor an outreach event for you to invite your friends to.

The big event had finally arrived. A world-class evangelistic speaker was coming in for several days. We had booked a couple of hot Christian bands. We had gotten all the campus Christian groups behind us and had also recruited a number of churches to work with us. We were prepared, prayed up and poised for a great evangelistic victory on a large Midwestern campus.

The evening of our first outreach meeting finally arrived. As we looked out over the great hall we had booked, we couldn't help feeling a wave of disappointment. Out of the forty thousand students on this campus, only about 550 had shown up. And most of these were already Christians. The band did well, but the world-class evangelistic speaker, though full of energy and enthusiasm, used some Christian lingo and a preaching style that did not win over the crowd. His style was authoritarian. He had the answer; non-Christians didn't. They needed Jesus. Though this fine preacher expressed the truths of the gospel, his language, style and approach were off-putting for many students.

Each of the following three nights the crowds grew a little, reaching about eleven hundred the last night. But still the overwhelming majority were Christian. About fifty people registered decisions for Christ that week. Many of these people had actually been reached mainly through Bible studies and other outreach events in dorms. We had spent nearly sixty thousand dollars and had logged thousands of hours of preparation and prayer. We had hoped to see a major breakthrough for the gospel on that campus. The outcome wasn't anything close to what we had hoped for and prayed for.

I felt like a failure. Many of us did. Had we heard God wrong? Why weren't people more interested in Jesus? Why had the speaker been so poorly received?

Initially I decided to give up on large event evangelism. I still had great passion to reach people outside God's family, but I was discouraged. I didn't think it was possible to do it. And so my passion and vision gradually diminished, and I began to turn my heart and attention to other things.

Has your church or ministry ever sponsored a seeker event but seen very few pre-Christians attend? In your personal conversations or invitations have you struggled with people's apparent lack of interest in Jesus? Have you gotten fired up about reaching people outside God's family but then seen your enthusiasm gradually dissipate, with little real impact?

Many of us feel that way. Our friends just don't seem that interested. The outreach events sponsored by our church or ministry don't seem to draw many seekers. Over time, as we see so little fruitfulness in our witness, we get discouraged. We give up. We would never say that we've given up, but that is what has happened in our hearts. We might read books. We might try new strategies here and there. But we're just not that excited about evangelism anymore.

This book assumes that you want to reach those outside God's family but may not be seeing as much progress as you might hope. If you knew what to do, you would do it. But nothing seems to work very well, and when you see very little progress you just can't seem to maintain your passion. If you really saw some approach that would bear fruit among your friends and that you felt able to do with God's help, you would go for it in a moment.

Breaking Open the Box

A few years ago I began to experience a revolution in the way I viewed and did evangelism. This revolution helped me identify the boxes I had put God in and the boxes I had put around evangelism. This revolution is built on understanding people today and the ways they think about life and spiritual issues. This revolution is based on hearing and understanding their questions more deeply, learning how people today come to know and love Jesus. I began to see more fruit in my life, and I began to visit and learn from other ministries that were seeing a lot of people come home to God.

I have gotten so excited about evangelism. I am optimistic and hopeful, and my vision and passion don't leak away as they used to. But it is not evangelism the way I used to do it. It is not the same evangelism that I practiced for that big event that went so poorly. It is evangelism outside the box. It is evangelism that helps people *experience* the good news in new ways. It is evangelism in the power of God's Spirit, in the context of community, that is effective at speaking to people's questions *today!*

Are you interested in learning more and in viewing and doing evangelism in new ways? Do you feel a need to get out of your own boxes and see God do some new things in reaching people outside the family through you? Then I invite you to come along on the adventure of understanding people better, of hearing some powerful and exciting ways God is at work in our day, and of letting God lead you outside of your boxes in order to reach many more people than you have ever been able to reach before!

At the end of the book is a list of sources cited, which serves as a good reading list as well. You'll come across references to these works throughout the book. I give you the author's name and any appropriate page numbers in the text; you'll find the rest of the information you'll need at the end of the book.

As you work through this book and discuss it with others, my hope is that you grow in urgency, expectancy and excitement and that you see a steadily growing stream of people being spiritually reborn through your life and outreach. Do you want that? Then let's jump in!

Discussion Questions

1. Look at Luke 15. What do you notice about Jesus' heart and priorities? What do you notice about the value of the things lost, the urgency of the search and the response when what was lost is found? How does that

encourage and challenge you?

2. How would you rank your heart for reaching people outside the family of God? Is your passion high? Why or why not? What might help you grow in sharing God's heart for those outside his family?

3. Have you ever helped plan an outreach event that didn't go well? What happened? How did it affect you?

4. What do you hope you get out of reading this book? Take a moment to pray and ask God to use this book in your life.

1

WHAT'S OUR BOX?

WE WANT TO SEE PEOPLE COME TO KNOW JESUS. WE WANT TO SEE PEOPLE IN heaven with God forever. We want to see people become devoted followers of Jesus Christ. That's what you and I long for. That's why you're reading this book. You and I won't be satisfied until God's hand is stretched out and we're seeing more fruitfulness.

This chapter is about identifying and taking down barriers—old ways of viewing and doing evangelism. If we don't first understand what's holding us back, we won't be ready to embrace important new ideas.

Often when we start to make witness a passion and a priority, we run into a major barrier: our "boxes," mental models of ministry and evangelism that keep us from pouring our passion into new ways of witness. If we are growing in our passion for witness but pouring our efforts and energy into the same structures and strategies we've always had, we will see little increase in fruitfulness. After a time we will get discouraged and our passion will disappear.

How do we get in touch with our boxes, the mental models and unspoken rules that keep us from bearing more and better fruit?

The Shattering of a Box

Here's how I was pushed out of my box. One year I took eleven students from the University of Wisconsin-Madison InterVarsity ministry to leadership and planning camp. I was their staff pastor. We were fired up, we were excited, we had a lot of vision. Our ministry had grown from sixty-five to seventy-five that year. We had eleven high-quality student leaders planning and praying and dreaming about what God wanted us to do. We felt pretty good about ourselves and our ministry.

We started to meet, and we were getting some good vision, beginning to think about drawing in new students. We made some plans and began to assign jobs. We had two small group coordinators. We designated two large group coordinators, an administrator, a prayer person, an evangelism person, a publicity person. We had people assigned according to gifts, and we were ready to roll!

Then we made a fatal mistake. At least it was fatal to our self-satisfaction. We asked a friend from the Navigators ministry to come in and consult with us. He came into that group of eleven leaders, and he asked a bunch of good leadership questions. "What's your vision? What's your strategy? What's your plan? What are your roles?"

About ten minutes into the discussion, he stopped. He got really quiet. He said, "Now let me get this straight. You've got a ministry with seventy-five students involved?"

"Yeah, we've been growing!"

"You've got eleven really good student leaders here?" he asked.

"Yeah, aren't they great?"

"And you're using those eleven good student leaders to run a ministry of seventy-five. Is that what I'm hearing? Now I heard you're going to collect a few pre-Christians. I heard that. But mostly, these eleven people are running this ministry of seventy-five, meeting the needs of the people you already have, plus the needs of some Christian freshmen that you will collect? I'm just trying to make sure I'm hearing you right."

"Yeah, I guess so." We were becoming a little less enthusiastic in our responses.

Then he pounced! "Man, two or three of you could run this ministry, no sweat. Take eight of you and go do something for God, for goodness sake!"

We protested: "What do you mean, 'go do something for God'? We're reaching out to new students, we've got large groups going, we've got a bunch of small groups going, we're working at integrating our faith and our practice, and we're doing something for God! What do you mean, 'go do something for God'?"

He continued pressing. "You know, all that stuff is great; that's in the Bible, OK. But if you guys aren't extending the kingdom and reaching those outside God's family and bringing in more people to become followers of Jesus, then you might as well fold your tent and go home!"

Whoa! I was ticked! Eleven of us walked out of there ticked. We spent the night ticked. The next morning we were still ticked.

That afternoon we started to get convicted. That evening we found ourselves confessing, repenting and letting God lead us out of our boxes. We chose three of our ministry leaders and said, "OK, you three are going to do something for God. You're going to run our ministry of seventy-five." The remaining eight of us then agreed, "We are *really* going to go take a risk together for God. We're going to reach that dorm complex that we've never touched, where all the party freshmen live. We don't relate to them that well, but we're going to learn, and we're going to go reach them for Jesus."

The eight of us didn't do any administration for the ministry of the seventy-five for the entire year. We became an outreach team to reach people in a dorm complex. On the first three days of school we helped first-year students move in, did surveys to explore spiritual interest and asked if people were interested in Bible study. We got forty interested first-year students. We started eight groups, mostly with pre-Christian students. We looked at the life of Jesus for six weeks. Then we trained our leaders to lead people to Christ. The leaders went to their groups, shared the gospel and asked people to commit themselves to Christ. A few responded.

Then we took the whole bunch of Bible study attenders on a retreat. Every winter we'd had a retreat with twenty people in our group attending—a really fuzzy, warm, wonderful retreat. This year we had seventy-five, forty of them pre-Christian, and they showed it! Many were smoking, swearing, playing cards, hanging out and being themselves—and being accepted.

Now the nuns who administered the retreat center weren't quite so happy with us. They kept looking everywhere to find out who was in charge. And every time I saw them coming I would duck behind somebody.

At one point I think I grabbed a cigarette to blend in. They weren't going to find out who was in charge if I could help it!

The final session was powerful, as the Holy Spirit worked to invite a lot of these students into the kingdom. At least thirty of the students responded.

Let me tell you, the ministry of seventy-five was run just fine, and we added about thirty-five or forty to become a ministry of about 120 in that year. Nearly thirty of the new members were also new Christians! I was so glad my Navigator friend had ticked us off and didn't just let us do business as usual and stay in the box.

One reason for our new levels of fruitfulness was the dedication of more than half of our people and material resources to reaching those outside God's family. As many of us have discovered, it takes a disproportionate commitment for evangelism to reach the level of intensity of other values and priorities. What will it take for you and your church?

Again and again I've seen students, ministry staff and church people get passionate for witness, wanting to share God's heart, wanting to reach those outside God's family; then they'll share their plans, and it looks to me like the same plan I've seen about 100,000 other times. We're too often trapped in boxes that keep us from seeing God and what he wants to do today.

What are the boxes for your church or ministry? What are the boxes that keep you from being fruitful and effective in witness?

I want to share thoughts about the boxes I've seen in ministries and churches over the years. As I expose these boxes, think about what your boxes might be and how you can begin to let God open you up to new ways of reaching out to the people around you.

But watch out. Identifying the mental pictures of the way we view and do evangelism is hard work. It will call us to make challenging changes. As a result, we will face intense spiritual warfare aimed at keeping us in the same boxes, keeping us largely ineffective and fruitless.

Like Paul, we need to fight this battle with weapons that have divine power to demolish strongholds. We are to demolish arguments and every pretension that sets itself up against the knowledge of God, and we are to take captive every thought to make it obedient to Christ. Our battle is for truth and for more fruitful mental models of ministry and evangelism. Our spiritual warfare is against arguments and ways of viewing and doing evangelism that are actually pretensions that keep us from obedience to Christ.

These old beliefs and practices represent the ways we violate God's heart and God's command to reach the lost (Mt 15:3). They are unintended barriers we put in front of people that keep them from coming home to God.

Did you ever realize there is a great spiritual battle around the way you and your ministry view and do evangelism? So much is at stake!

Our Theology Box
First, we have mental models and theological notions about evangelism that keep us (and God) in a box.

We often say that God is responsible for conversion. We are responsible only to be faithful. So faithfulness, not fruitfulness, should be our focus.

The truth in that idea is that only God can bring the rebirth of a soul. But God uses us as collaborators. God is the ultimate source of the "catch," but if we are using the wrong bait or fishing in a stagnant lake or using poor fishing methods, we won't catch anything.

It is not that evangelism is 100 percent God's activity and 0 percent ours. It's not even a fifty-fifty deal. Evangelism is 100 percent both: 100 percent God and 100 percent us. That is the mystery of the incarnation, how God came to us in Jesus. Jesus was 100 percent God and 100 percent human. That is the way God works through his church. He fills 100 percent human beings with his 100 percent divine Holy Spirit. That is the way God's work and witness in the world goes forward.

The people who put all their eggs in the basket of prayer and spiritual warfare and sit around until God shows up in some future event are living out a superspiritual or anti-incarnational approach to evangelism. They think it's all God and we're just along to worship and pray.

The people who ignore prayer and believe that the right methods will automatically produce the right results can be worldly and are also anti-incarnational in approach and theology.

Unbalanced Calvinism—the idea that it all depends on God—is deadly to evangelism. So is unbalanced Arminianism—the idea that it all depends on us.

It's both. It's incarnational, the right human means indwelt by the Spirit of God. Prayer *and* action. Faithfulness *and* fruitfulness. Faithfulness without fruitfulness is an oxymoron in a biblical, incarnational life.

Let's let God lead us out of the box in our theology, our view of God!

Pray your heart out. Do so individually. Do so corporately. Ask God to show you the spiritual barriers to evangelism on your campus, in your community and in your hearts. Satan trembles when we pray! Listen to God about who you're to reach, who you're to pray for and even heal.

But don't just pray. Act. Act now! Learn from the best, most fruitful evangelism ministries you can find. Adapt their strategies. Don't merely adopt their methods. That is a sure-fire way to diminish, not increase, your fruitfulness. Don't try to be a carbon copy of some other successful ministry. But give your best thought and energy and resources and time to developing ministry and training people to reach those outside God's family in your sphere of influence.

It's 100 percent God.

It's 100 percent you and your people.

It's the incarnation, God's filling and blessing the right human means. It is human beings seeing what God is doing and jumping in with both feet and with committed hearts and with busy hands and mouths.

May God lead us out of our theological boxes.

Our Sacred Practices Box

Every ministry and stream of tradition in the church has a great strength that can ultimately become its constricting box.

For my own ministry, InterVarsity, it is the analytical, thoughtful, critical, autonomous spirit that God has used mightily in our books and publications and in our engagement with university students and faculty. Unfortunately, we have often analyzed until we are paralyzed! Our meetings sometimes seem cold and unwelcoming. We are more likely to have dark reflective lighting for our group spaces. Some of us may not blink an eye when we host hour-long biblical expositions at our meetings, camps and conferences. Some of us would lay down our lives to have students sing complicated ancient hymns. In these ways we can be more and more out of touch with students today. These things are changing about us. And there are those among us who are too willing to throw out the traditions that have given us life. But we have to face in a clear-eyed way how pre-Christians feel when they visit us.

I am watching a couple of national campus ministries explode with evangelistic fruitfulness. My own ministry is seeing some progress, but we long for so much more. I believe one reason we are seeing so much less than we long for is our sacred practices box. How do we maintain and pass on our great strength of growing the mind of Christ in people, but reinvent practices that build better bridges to people today? We need to have light-filled, energetic spaces. We need to embrace experiences and reflect on them a little less quickly and skeptically, though in the end not less deeply. We can actually trust the Holy Spirit to guide us through those experiences. We need to address issues not just of thinking but also of feeling and imagining and committing in ways that people today can engage with and be intrigued by. Transforming today's experience-oriented people into critical, analytical people is not always the same thing as helping them to become more like Jesus!

I'm not just thinking of my own ministry. Every group begun before the late 1960s is probably wired up to reach the more thoughtful, individualistic, scientific kind of person who trusts in logic and evidence and cares about truth. Most people today are more experience-oriented, hungry for community and concerned about personal but not absolute truth. Many today don't even believe absolute truth exists; most are sure that even if absolute truth exists, no one group or person has it. Our boxes can keep us from reaching those often spiritually seeking people. Every ministry born in the 1960s or before probably needs significant and sometimes painful soul-searching and change, especially in the area of its sacred practices, in order to thrive and be fruitful today. We struggle to commit to these changes, fearing that if we give up certain sacred practices and strategies, we will lose our purpose, orthodoxy and identity and cease to please God.

But there is a way out of our dilemma: distinguishing between our core values and our sacred practices. We need to embrace and hold on to core values. We want people to know the Scriptures, to think with the mind of Christ, to love God with heart, mind, soul and strength, to love their neighbors as themselves. But churches' and ministries' ways of fulfilling their core values may have worked in the past but may be holding them back from reaching people in the present.

For liturgical churches the sacred practice can be the liturgy and the sacraments. The altar becomes the be-all and the end-all. Services have to look the same every week. If we can't get to the core value of symbol and ceremony and then reinvent ways for pre-Christians to enter in, we will never reach them. The liturgy will be an unintelligible mystery. That's not all bad. Mystery is very attractive to people today. But there must be events and entry points that *are* intelligible and meet felt needs. Liturgical churches seem to be very weak at creating and hosting spiritual interest-generating events and at speaking relevantly to pre-Christian people. Of course there are many times to let fly with the liturgy and to celebrate it in all its tradition and pomp and mystery. But we cannot let the liturgy become a barrier to the pre-Christian coming in, as Israel's temple practices could be for non-Jews.

For some churches the hour-long expository sermon is the sacred practice that cannot be touched. Unfortunately, pre-Christian people today will listen to maybe one speaker in a million for that long and return again. Aren't there ways to teach the Bible that are more interactive, that foster dialogue and experiential learning, that help people enter into the Scriptures imaginatively? Can't we at least take a Sunday a month and devote it to experimenting with communicating the Scriptures in a way pre-Christian people today can respond to?

For some charismatic churches, intense, heartfelt, very intimate worship is the sacred and untouchable practice. Worship can be great evangelism. But it probably will not be attractive to pre-Christians if everybody looks like they are immersed in a very private experience, and if people are expressing their exuberance in strange ways.

Our sacred practice likely expresses our greatest strength, the greatest gift we have to give. So we don't just drop it. Instead we identify the core value and adjust the practice to fulfill the core value but not alienate the pre-Christian.

Of course in some of our gatherings we will continue to focus on mature Christians, and here we can be free to carry out the sacred practice in those old and powerful ways. What's more, as long as we are communicating and caring well, ancient practices and the experience of the transcendent and mysterious are immensely attractive to people today.

What are your sacred practices? Can you identify them? What keeps pre-Christian people repulsed or indifferent when they visit your gatherings?

What are the core values that lie behind your sacred practices? How can you express those values and instill them without becoming irrelevant and incomprehensible to pre-Christians today?

This may be our greatest spiritual battle. Many of us feel like we are in a fight to the death to maintain sacred practices that are gradually losing their power and relevance in our world. Our tendency is to battle harder, to hold on tighter, to exhort and plead, to weep and cry out. There is certainly a need for prophets who call us back to the ancient ways. But there is also great need for evangelists who will translate core values into new practices that will resonate with and reach pre-Christian people. Often, sad to say, the prophets and evangelists spend a lot of time beating each other up!

Our Structure and Strategy Box

Much teaching on evangelism tells us that relationships matter but our structures and strategies don't. If we just love people, any structure or strategy will do. This just isn't true.

If evangelism is a once-a-year structure or strategy for our ministry, our people will consider it a once-a-year priority and not an ongoing lifestyle.

If Christian members are overwhelmed with activities with other Christians, and we have helped create that structure and pattern, with our words we are saying one thing—that lost people matter to God—and with our structures and priorities we are saying another thing—that lost people are not a priority.

If a church or ministry can be considered successful whether or not it is experiencing growth through new conversions and commitments to Christ, then new conversions and commitments will not really become a priority. How many times do we say, "We don't just want to take people from other ministries and shift the sheep around. We want to reach the unchurched"? Then we blithely go ahead and shift the sheep around. If our ministry grows, most people will tell us we have been successful, whether or not we have grown merely by shifting sheep.

I love what Campus Crusade, a ministry reaching college students, did in 1991-1992. They were not reaching those outside the Christian family very effectively, even though they were still counting lots of decisions for Christ, lots of staff and lots of Christians involved. Steve Sellers, campus ministry director, believed that Crusade's modernist, individualist, competitive approach was bearing less and less fruit. So the ministry decided to restate its mission: to turn lost students into Christ-centered laborers. That restatement got the focus in the right place. And then Crusade changed what it counted. Basically, the only figure that was valued as absolutely crucial, that was counted and reported constantly, had to do with the growth that came from new conversions and commitments to Christ. How many people are substantially involved in the ministry who weren't Christian when they started at the

campus? That's what Crusade counted. How many people became committed to Christ through their ministry, entered into Christian community and
were growing? The staff person I recently talked with wasn't sure how many
decisions for Christ the organization had counted that year, but he could tell
me the figures for growth in the number of new Christians now involved in
Christian community going back seven years.

To meet the primary goal of this kind of effective evangelism and
growth, many Campus Crusade groups have adapted their large group
meetings to make them high-energy, laughter-loving, welcoming events
that are fabulous for freshmen. And then they have focused most of their
energy on getting these students into small groups, where they come to
know Christ and come home to God.

They changed their mission. They changed what they counted. They
changed their structures. They are seeing God work in miraculous and
explosive ways. They model a change process many of us need. They let
God lead them out of their structure and strategy box.

One key issue in how we formulate our structure and our strategy is
where we start our planning and dreaming. Do we start with who we are
and figure out what we can do to reach people? If so, we often end up asking the pre-Christian to adapt her needs to our structures. Or do we look at
who the pre-Christian is and what it will take to reach her? If we start with
this question, we are pushed to adapt our strategy to her needs and let go of
structures and strategies that exclude her. In chapters three and four you
will get a lot of help in understanding how to think like the person you are
trying to reach and to adapt your structure and strategy accordingly.

So let's ask ourselves: What structure and strategy are we using to reach
pre-Christian people? How often do we reach out with our group meetings? How many of our leaders are focused on witness? How much of our
resources do we spend on witness? Are we really reaching the lost, or are
we competing for the found?

Be ruthlessly honest here. What are you really spending and doing in
order to reach the lost? Where are your people, time and money resources
allocated? Could you focus 40 percent of your leaders and resources and
church or group gatherings on witness? Evangelism is not the only thing or
even necessarily the most important thing. But it takes a disproportionate
investment of time, resources and energy to bring the value of evangelism
to equal footing with other values.

Just begin to dream about the radical difference those choices might make. Just begin to imagine the radical joy God will have, and will share with you, if you will seek him and those outside his family.

Our Self-Perception Box
Here are comments I've heard over the years from many people:

☐ Evangelism is for extroverts. It also helps if you're at least a little obnoxious. I am not an extrovert. And I'm just not comfortable being obnoxious.

☐ I will live my life, and when people ask me questions, only then will I share my faith.

☐ It is manipulative and underhanded of me to build a relationship only to share the gospel.

☐ I am not gifted in evangelism. I have other gifts, but not much role in witness.

☐ Evangelism is for superstars like Billy Graham, whom I could never be like.

☐ Evangelism is for obnoxious people like Brother So-and-So on the corner, whom I would never want to be like.

Earlier evangelism models emphasized reasoned preaching and explanation, best done by the professional. In our world today (and maybe even in the past too!), the story of a fellow friend is far more persuasive.

Evangelism is for all of us. I know introverts who have led more people to Christ than I have as an extrovert. Each of us has a style, giftedness and passion that can help the church in witness. As we become teams together, each of us can help all of us reach people today.

Think about it. You know people who can only be reached by a person just like you!

When you hear the word *evangelism,* don't think Billy Graham or Brother So-and-So. Think *you!* You will get more help in doing so in the chapter on evangelism in and through teams (chapter five).

So let me deal with more of the objections I listed above—objections that you yourself may have voiced or felt.

It is not manipulative to build a friendship with the goal of sharing Christ. It is loving, as long as we stay committed to our friends whether they respond to our appeal or not.

It is right to live our lives in ways that engender interest and questions from others. But we are not to wait passively until people ask questions. We can engage them actively, asking questions ourselves and sharing our lives and our stories of God at work. One of my friends calls this practice "living out loud." After all, how will people hear unless someone is sent who has the guts to share (Rom 10:14-15)?

A Story and a Challenge

I was traveling around to different campuses speaking at InterVarsity group meetings, and for a while those efforts were quite fruitful, but then I began to see a decrease in people responding. Finally I led two evangelistic meetings at which not a single person committed his or her life to Christ.

I was kind of scratching my head, thinking, *This fits with what I think, because evangelism is a process today, and people don't respond to thoughtful appeals to the mind and will.* I was falling into the box of thinking God could never work like he used to! And I was convincing myself to be happy with not seeing anybody come to know Jesus.

Then somebody confronted me: "You know, Rick, I don't think you have any faith for people to come to trust Christ at these things. Don't even go if you haven't prayed in faith that someone will come to know Jesus!"

I was convicted. I started praying every day, "God, I want to see people come to know Jesus. I want to see people come home to you!"

At my next campus event I did a mediocre job of giving an evangelistic message. It wasn't awful, but it certainly wasn't great. I got done and thought, *Oh well, that was OK.* And I gave an invitation: Anybody want to come to know Jesus?

Ten people said, "Yeah!" And we followed those ten people up, and it was all genuine. We often have not because we ask not.

Here's the bottom line: Ask God to help you personally lead someone to Christ this next year. I think God would be delighted if you wouldn't rest or stop praying until God let you lead somebody to Christ.

People have all kinds of reasons that undermine their faith for God to use them in this way: "I don't have that gift." "I stumble over my words." I had great reasons for why nobody came to Christ after my campus talks.

God has to give you the faith to pray for new conversions and commitments. I can't give it to you. You can't just work it up. But nothing would affect you or your ministry more then letting God lead you out of the box personally first. Let God fill you and use you to lead a friend to Christ, and you'll never want to go back into the box again!

Discussion Questions

1. How much time, energy and resources have you and your ministry focused on evangelism? How could you change that percentage? Could you give 40 percent to reaching those outside God's family? What might that look like? There is no magic number, but thinking in such terms could help you bring the same level of creativity and dedication to evangelism that your other priorities enjoy.

2. What boxes do you think you might have? What theological boxes? What sacred practices boxes? What structure and strategy boxes? What personal perception boxes?

3. What box do you think it is most critical for you to work on next? What steps do you need to take? Go back to that section in this chapter and work through the questions it poses. For instance, if you want to work on the sacred practices box, identify your sacred practice, then identify the core value behind the sacred practice, and then imagine a practice that can affirm your core value but not alienate pre-Christian people.

4. Could you begin to pray daily, and ask God for faith, that you would be used by God to lead someone to Christ over the next year? One woman challenged me recently: "Why don't we pray for God to let us lead *ten* people to Christ?"! I told her to go for it! What is God giving you the faith to ask for?

2

UNDERSTANDING TODAY'S QUESTIONS

NOW THAT WE HAVE BEGUN TO IDENTIFY OUR BOXES, WE ARE READY TO HEAR and respond to the new ways people are thinking and the new questions they are asking. We are ready to let them out of our boxes, our old conceptions of them, and invite them home to God.

What questions did people ask in the past? How did we answer them? Here's a story of a classic encounter I had some years ago, one that captures the kinds of questions and answers that used to satisfy most seeking people.

The Logic of Evidence

I got together with Debbie in Witte Dorm on the University of Wisconsin-Madison campus. I had met her the first week of school, and she had shown mild interest in Christian faith.

Debbie was an engineering student. As we talked, I learned she was in pain. Two of her closest friends had been killed in a car accident her senior year of high school. "Why did that have to happen? Why wasn't it me? I was supposed to be with them that night. I miss them so much! How can God be good and let that kind of thing happen?"

I felt her deep sadness. I wanted to give her an answer that would explain it all, but I couldn't, and I told her so.

As we got to know each other, I began to share how my faith had helped me in times of pain. She was interested but felt Christian faith was a crutch for mindless people. Yet she didn't think I was mindless. She just couldn't figure out how I could swallow that religious stuff.

I explained that I had felt that way too. And then I had met a guy on my campus who challenged me. He was thoughtful and caring, and I was attracted by his winsome personality. He also seemed to have some reasons for believing. He claimed he had evidence for his beliefs. I challenged him: "Prove it!" And he did, at least enough to get me to take a new look at Jesus.

Debbie was intrigued. "What proof?" she shot back.

"Well, I could talk about evidence that makes God's existence likely, or evidence that supports the reliability of the Bible. But here's the stuff that got to me. This guy claimed Jesus came back to life from the dead, and that he lives today to have a relationship with me. And then he went on to give me some great evidence."

"Really? What was it?" she demanded.

"Here's the heart of it. The followers of Jesus turned the Roman world upside down based on one simple message: 'Jesus was dead and now he's alive.' Now, I wasn't there. But they were. They were in a position to know beyond a shadow of doubt whether that message was true or not."

"Wait a minute. Maybe they saw what they wanted to see," she challenged.

"But look here," I came back at her, and I showed her 1 Corinthians 15:3-8. "Over five hundred people at one time saw Jesus alive after he had died. And when 1 Corinthians was written they were still around to confirm or deny the claim." Then I showed her the story of Thomas, who had to see and touch to believe.

"OK," she admitted, "so there's more to it than just the wishful thinking or hallucinations of a few people. Maybe they plotted it. They'd lost their leader and their power. So they stole the body and claimed he was still around."

"Good thought," I replied, "but not good enough!" By that time Debbie and I were pretty comfortable with each other. "These people died for that simple message. People will preach a lie. But will they die for a lie? Ten of the twelve main followers of Jesus died a painful death because of their message. No way would they do that if their message was false and they knew it."

Debbie continued to grill me. She squirmed and came up with every possible alternative explanation. We looked at the theory that Jesus didn't die but only passed out. We looked at the idea that maybe the Romans stole the body, or maybe the Jews stole it. In the end, she recognized that the life of those early followers of Jesus just couldn't be explained in any better way. Jesus must have come back from the dead!

"Does anybody else know about this?" she asked quietly. "Why, if this is true, this is big news! We have to get this out! Can we share this with some of my friends?"

"Well, sure," I responded.

That next week I returned to a full dorm room. Debbie had invited all the students from her floor and also all the other resident assistants in the dorm to hear the evidence for Jesus' coming back from the dead and being alive!

It was textbook. It was fun! This woman with a scientific view of truth and reality had looked the evidence in the eye, decided it was probably true, and couldn't wait to tell this incredible news to all of her friends.

Debbie cared a lot about historical and scientific evidence. She believed that logic worked in the area of spiritual issues. She was convinced by good evidence and couldn't wait to tell others. Once convinced, she moved toward a faith commitment. In her mind, if Jesus had risen from the dead, that made all the difference.

Well, I was jazzed!

A Quantum-Level Shift

I hoped that I could see this kind of response multiplied across that campus and on many other campuses. But a few years later I ran into a very different student with some very different questions. This next encounter encapsulates the earthquake-level change in culture and people's questions that we have been going through for some time now. Bob had a very different response to my evidence, logic and appeal to absolutes.

Bob was a philosophy of science student at the University of Illinois. I had met him through one of the women in my campus group. She was practicing "dating evangelism"! So she begged me to help her by meeting him. I sought him out when I went to visit his campus.

I went into the time with Bob loaded for bear. Bob was going to hear this great news, look at this great evidence, become a Christian and then invite all his science-type friends to come and hear the evidence. It worked with Debbie. Why couldn't it work with Bob? Same news. Same evidence. But oh, such a different response!

I told Bob about my fabulous time with Debbie and asked if he wanted to hear the evidence that made such an impact on her. "Sure," he replied. "Give it your best shot."

"Well," I began, "there's a lot of evidence that Jesus rose from the dead. And if he rose from the dead, then he's alive today and available to be in a relationship with us."

That's all I got out. Then Bob took me on a wild ride through the developments in science that have drastically changed the way we look at the world.

"Rick, let me play with your mind a little bit. Will you let me do that first? Then I'd be glad to hear your evidence."

"Sure," I naively replied.

"Albert Einstein. You've heard of him, right?" He was baiting me. No doubt about it.

"Well, yeah," I responded.

"Einstein showed us that time and space are not absolutes but relative to each other, that matter and energy are interchangeable, that space is curved, and that what you see depends on your frame of reference. Right?"

"Right!" I replied enthusiastically, trying to make it sound like I was ahead of him here.

"So scientific truth is relative to the frame of reference of the observer. So is any other sort of truth, in my thinking," he concluded. "Thus your evidence for the resurrection of Jesus is evidence you can see from your frame of reference. That's all it is." He didn't seem to need a response, which was good. I couldn't quite think of one.

"Can I go on?" he asked.

"Why not?" I replied, though I could think of some pretty good reasons why not.

"Have you heard of Niels Bohr, Max Planck and Werner Heisenberg?"

He wasn't baiting me anymore, just pressing forward.

"I've heard of them," I responded, though at that point I could have told you more about the Three Stooges than those three scientists. All my knowledge had come from Frank Herbert, the science-fiction writer of *Dune*.

"They are quantum theorists, scientists who have mapped out a whole new vision of reality. They and others have shown us that there is a lower limit to our abilities to measure things. They have shown us that light is both wave and particle. They have shown us that when we measure reality at the smallest level, there is only probability. Do you know what this means?" He was getting excited, and I was getting lost.

"You tell me." I wanted to put the ball right back in his court on this one!

"Quantum theory has immense consequences for our view of reality." He was definitely getting evangelistic. "First, logic can no longer be seen as either-or. Either Christianity is true or it's false. Reality is also-and. Light is a wave and it's also a particle. So when you give me your arguments, you're operating with that old-time dichotomizing logic that went out with the downfall of Isaac Newton's world of simple, certain scientific truth. Logic is synthetic. It creates contradiction in order to achieve a new and greater synthesis.

"Second, all reality is participant reality. There is no such thing as an independent, objective world that you can observe without changing. You can't measure light particles without changing them, without creating the reality you observe. You probably want to make me think that the early Christians just reported the historical facts."

I didn't say a word.

"They helped create the facts they observed, and then reported them out of their interpretation of reality. Scientists do that. Writers do that. Religious people like you do that.

"Third," he went on, "uncertainty and chaos rule the behavior of life at the small and individual level. Patterns only emerge at the macro level, and those patterns are complicated and beautiful. Your simple explanation of life in black and white is too easy. It erases the complexity and imposes authority on life that is fundamentally spontaneous, a world of probability and playfulness.

"So," he concluded, "give me your evidence. I'd love to hear it now."

"Well, I have to go; my ride is waiting. But I'd love to meet again," I replied, muttering under breath, "maybe after I get my Ph.D." Clearly I had some homework to do!

I have come to love knee-jerk relativists, people who pick and choose their beliefs as if they were the creator of their own universe. I talked with one such fellow recently at a nearby college. I asked him what he believed God was like. He told me he thought God was like an emerging consciousness, the soul of the universe. I told him, "That's one view of God. Another is that God created the universe and is somehow in the universe but also still separate from it."

His response, without batting an eye: "Oh, I believe that too." Our culture and our campuses today are filled with such relativists. But Bob wasn't like that. Profound changes in the ways scientists are seeing the world are radically transforming our basic picture. The world is a process, a participant reality, the spontaneous emergence of one possibility out of immeasurable probability. This universe is only one universe out of innumerable alternate probability universes that may exist somewhere and somewhen.

Pain and Resistance

The day after I talked with Bob, I ran into Melissa. I asked her, after learning she was not open to Christian faith, what her biggest barrier to faith was. She responded, "That awful chauvinist St. Paul."

"Well, you know, he was way ahead of his day on women's rights," I responded. "He was trying to manage slow change because he wanted the Christians to bring people from the culture along. But he believed deeply in the gifts and leadership of women and worked closely with folk like an early church leader named Priscilla. The irony is that the church later ignored Paul's spirit of supporting and managing change and froze his specific advice into universal rules."

"Yeah, they sure did," she responded. "The church is so oppressive to women, so white-male-run, so demeaning and controlling toward the identity and freedom of women. You all try to legislate our lives. What gives you the right?" At this point Melissa's voice was raised. This was not an academic issue to her. And clearly I was partly responsible, in her mind. And if the truth be told, in ways I wasn't even aware of she was partly right. I was responsible, especially for my silence.

People in today's world are not going to let other people, people representing a very oppressive past, tell them who they are. For good reason.

Several years ago, at another college, I spoke on Romans 1, where Paul talks about the disintegration of society. In this passage Paul denounces homosexual relations as being a result of God's giving us up to our own sinful choices. Laura, from the gay and lesbian student group, was there. I will never forget her hurt, anger and fear at hearing me use this passage to tell her that she wasn't homosexual in her core identity. Homosexuality is not an identity that God either created or redeemed, I explained. It is a false identity.

However true to Scripture I had been that night, I realized that I had put another stake in Laura's heart. I wasn't starting in the right place for her. I was claiming the right to tell her who she is. That will not be received in a postmodern world. That cannot be where we start.

Sandy, another college student, brought that home to me recently. I started the conversation by asking what her religious background was and if it was still meaningful to her. I affirmed her as she shared her disillusionment with her background. Beginning to trust me, she started to express her hurt and anger at people who told others what to believe and who they were.

I asked Sandy if she was open to thinking about some of the evidence and argument for the credibility of the Christian worldview. Her response: "No, not really. Your evidence, your logic, all that is merely your attempt to feel good about who you are and what you believe. Your logic is an exercise in conquest. You want to prove your way of thinking and believing is right so that you can be in charge. Your logic is merely an exercise in your will to power. I frankly am not interested in your power. I want my own."

Peter Berger captures the style of witness that is dead for most people today: "A peculiar mixture of arrogance ('I know the truth') and benevolence ('I want to save you') has always been the chief psychological hallmark of missionary activity" (quoted in Pritchard, p. 126). People can smell this combination of arrogance and benevolence a mile away. At the first whiff they will fly away—miles away.

Inviting Without Arrogance
How do we model certainty without arrogance, compassion without condescension? It's not easy, but it can be done.

I saw a good example recently. Lee Strobel is a former pastor at Willow

Creek Community Church in Illinois and is now at Saddleback Church in southern California, a large and very evangelistic church. Lee is also the author of *The Case for Christ*. Speaking at the University of Wisconsin-Madison, he emphasized heavily the incredible odds against the fulfillment of all the Old Testament prophecies about Christ. For eight of them to be fulfilled in one person, Lee told us, the odds against that happening by chance are astronomical.

Lee offered the following analogy. "Take tiles the size of a quarter and tile this room, and then this campus, and then this city, and then this state, and then this country, and then all the land areas of the world, and put a gold X on the bottom of just one of those tiles. Now give your friend transportation, and as much time as he wants, send him all over the world, but tell him he can pick only one tile. The probability of all eight of those prophecies applying to one man by chance is the same probability that your friend will stoop down, pick up one tile and find on the bottom the one gold X you put there. It is far more likely that Jesus fulfilled those prophecies because he is who he said he is. But you decide."

Lee expressed certainty and yet allowed for choice. He was humorous in the process too. Because he had been an atheist, he didn't seem arrogant or benevolent in the way he communicated. Often he was pointing to evidence that had forced him to change his own mind when he was an atheist. He was a great storyteller too, and people today won't argue with our story.

Lee was a great model.

Entering a New World
After the meeting I ran into another common barrier, though. I sat with a fellow who had attended the talk and wanted me to take him through the prophecies. He was a literature major. I started with Isaiah 53, a passage that even many Jewish people have been convinced points toward Jesus' crucifixion. This postmodern lit major came up with fifteen different ways to interpret the passage, pointed to several different figures who might have fulfilled it, and then just came after me, demonstrating that I'd merely read the passage out of the interpretation of reality I already had. "You brought your answers with you, Rick. You only understand texts by entering into them and interpreting them out of your grid. Therefore your interpretation is not 'right' in some special way. You helped create the reality of the text by entering into it and interpreting it. Your prophecies proved what you

believe not because they really prove what you believe but because you went into the text already believing it! If that's the best proof you have, you're toast!"

All of us who name the name of Christ will need to do our homework. We do not need a Ph.D. to share Christ in a postmodern world with people like Bob, Laura, Sandy, Melissa and this lit major. But we have to understand the emerging sensibilities, the new shape of consciousness, the epochal shift in the questions people are asking. Some will respond to new renditions of old answers that satisfied people earlier. But many will not be so satisfied. We need to start at a different point with them. We need to enter their world, just as Jesus entered ours. We need to make sense to their sensibilities and communicate to their emerging consciousness.

Questions That Heat Up a Room

I recently attended a conference and served on a panel for a group of people that included young Christians and pre-Christians. They were given freedom to ask questions about the credibility of Christian faith. One person (planted by me!) asked about the evidence for the resurrection. Others asked about the reliability of the Bible. They seemed politely interested in our answers.

Then someone asked about homosexuality and how we can question homosexual identity and practice. The temperature in the room went up. A few tempers flared. At this point people were clearly not merely politely interested.

I have begun to use that experience to help me know when I am hearing the real and urgent questions of today's generation. What questions evoke their intensity and concern? When do they start to get offended? What questions hit them where they live? What questions are in the air that we breathe in our world today? When I hear those questions, I know I am beginning to tap into the hearts and minds and imaginations of people.

Here is a summary of some of the new questions we face, the questions that are in the very air that we breathe.

1. Questions of power and motive. Even our logical answers can feel like an exercise of colonializing power to people today. To many people we're just another tribe, using logic to gain power. Postmodern people have redefined truth as "whatever works for you, whatever rings true to your experience, whatever feels real to you." There is no "metanarrative," no grand story to inspire people, no explanation of everything. Any attempt to claim that one has the truth for everybody is experienced as an arrogant, offensive attempt at domination and control.

2. *Questions of identity.* Who am I? Who will I listen to for help in developing my identity and sense of self? How can you Christians think you can tell other people who they are? Each person has to create her own meaning and identity and align with others to increase her power base. After all, we're in a battle. We're a minority (whoever we are!). So who do you think you are to invalidate my sense of self and identity and my group's definition of who we are?

3. *Questions of pain and suffering.* Why do I hurt? Why did my family break apart? Why is there so much hatred and violence in the world? There is no grand story. People are crying out not so much for philosophical answers as for a way to give meaning and purpose to personal and corporate pain and suffering.

4. *Questions of character, trust and attractiveness.* Why should I trust you? Look at what believers have done. Racism. Sexism. Homophobia. The Crusades. Religious wars. Intolerance and dogmatic, narrow hate seem to mark your institutions. You are constantly drawing lines of exclusion. Your character is no better than the character of the society you live in. I can trust you just as much as I can trust other leaders in our society: hardly at all.

5. *Questions of love and meaning.* How can you reject the homosexual lifestyle? How can you say you love people when you reject who they are, how they define their very identity? How can you question living together when people love each other? How can you be rule-oriented in your ethics when the situation has to determine what is really loving and meaningful?

6. *Questions of interpretation.* Isn't the way you see the world completely dependent on your community and place of birth? Can't you interpret Scriptures any way you want, and haven't you? I don't care about the Bible's reliability. I am concerned about its integrity and moral value. After all, it was written by patriarchal, ethnocentric people.

7. *Questions of relevance and relativism.* Does your belief change lives? Does prayer really make a difference? Do you live a better or a happier life? Does your religion work? Does it help you with your pain? If it works for you, why should it work for me? What does it matter what you believe as long as it works and helps you? The question of the uniqueness of Christ is not primarily philosophical. It is a question about utility and relevance.

Don't all religions help people equally? If a religion works and feels real to a person, then it is true for that person. People are not looking for theological comparisons but for attractiveness, relevance and usefulness comparisons.

8. Questions of impact. Does your religion help society? Does it help me, whether I'm in your group or not? Or are you just another self-serving group? Of course you are.

How do we reach people asking these questions? How do we reach people today?

The next chapter will begin to look at how people come to faith in Christ today, what their process looks like, and how we can begin to answer the questions that are in the very air we breathe.

Discussion Questions

1. What are the questions your pre-Christian friends have about faith? When do they get offended? What questions really engage them?

2. How do you respond to their questions? How have they responded to your attempts to answer them? Do you feel prepared and equipped to respond to their questions? What would help you?

3. Do you agree that people's questions have changed? Why or why not?

4. Joint exercise: Go back to the conversations recounted in this chapter. Talk about how you would answer some of the questions I faced.

3

RESPONDING TO TODAY'S QUESTIONS

AS I ENCOUNTERED THE PEOPLE I TALKED ABOUT IN THE LAST CHAPTER, I WAS launched into a crisis. It was a crisis of inadequacy, of fear of rejection, and of feeling powerless to influence them toward Christ. They were asking questions I wasn't prepared to answer, and they no longer seemed interested in the questions I was prepared to answer.

Why weren't people responding to what I had responded to when I came to Christ? How would I answer their challenging questions? Did I need to get a Ph.D. in philosophy of science or quantum physics to talk to my friend Bob? Did I need a degree in postmodern literary theory to answer the lit major? Did I need to understand postmodern philosophy and theories of power, politics and identity in order to have anything to say to Laura, Melissa and Sandy, my feminist and gay friends? Why wasn't I seeing more people come into God's kingdom? Why weren't more people coming to our meetings or embracing our answers or responding to our challenge to come home to God? What were we doing wrong or not doing right? Is it all just in God's hands, so we ought to be happy with any fruit at all, no matter how meager?

Then I began to understand why people had these questions and what kind of response they would listen to. I realized that to respond to the new questions people are asking, I need to understand why they are asking those questions. I need to understand the cultural shift we are going through.

Tracking the Western Mind

I believe with many others that our culture is traveling through a shift in mindset that is epochal, a major earthquake in the mental landscape of our generation. Such a shattering shift may have occurred only three other times in the history of Western culture.

Richard Tarnas describes these past and current shifts in his book *The Passion of the Western Mind.* I have found many books to be helpful for delineating the transition from the modern to the postmodern world—for instance, Stan Grenz's *A Primer on Postmodernism* is excellent. But no book tells the story of epochal shifts in mindset in as compelling a way for me as Tarnas's.

Each major transition, Tarnas says, has been associated with a central figure who was in some sense martyred. Each great epochal transformation in the history of the Western mind appears to have been initiated by a sacrifice. As if to consecrate the birth of a fundamentally new cultural vision, in each case a symbolically resonant trial and martyrdom of some sort was suffered by its central prophet: the trial and execution of Socrates (469-399 B.C.) at the birth of the classical Greek mind, the trial and crucifixion of Jesus (4 B.C.-A.D. 29) at the birth of Christianity, and the trial and condemnation of Galilei Galileo (1564-1642) at the birth of modern science (Tarnas, p. 395).

These three epochs—classical, medieval and modern—were each marked by a certain mindset. Christian faith has had to address first the Greek mind, then the medieval mind and finally the modern scientific mind, for its proclamation to stay relevant and influence the hearts and minds of people.

Unfortunately, most of our approaches to proclaiming the gospel are still aimed at the modern scientific, analytical, individualistic mindset. We are ineffective in part because we are building our communication bridge to a mindset and an age that are passing away, or at least being radically transformed.

We need to understand and address a new mindset if our proclamation and demonstration of the gospel are to remain relevant and influence the minds and hearts of the next generation. The emerging mindset has been labeled "postmodern." Tarnas explains:

> By all accounts the central prophet of the postmodern mind was Friedrich Nietzsche (1844-1900). And we see a curious, perhaps aptly postmodern analogy of this theme of sacrifice and martyrdom with the extraordinary inner trial and imprisonment—the intense intellectual ordeal, the extreme psychological isolation, and the eventually paralyzing madness—suffered at the birth of the postmodern by Nietzsche, who signed his last letters "The Crucified," and who died at the dawn of the 20th century. (p. 395)

I won't attempt in this short chapter to do full justice to this epochal shift. Appendix one provides a discussion of how some of the themes of postmodernism developed. Here we will focus on a few dimensions of this shift that will help us immensely in responding to the questions people are asking today.

Setting the Stage: The Modern Mindset

To begin grasping the dimensions of today's cultural shift, we need to briefly summarize the modern mindset that used to guide the questions people had and the answers that satisfied them.

The modern mindset was born in the Enlightenment with people like Isaac Newton (1642-1727), René Descartes (1596-1650) and Francis Bacon (1561-1626).

Bacon, in England, helped develop one great principle of knowledge that drove the Enlightenment: the principle of empiricism expressed in the inductive method. The first foundation of knowledge is the senses. The key activity of the knower is observation and collection of data through the senses.

Descartes, a French philosopher, developed the Enlightenment's other great principle of knowledge: rationalism. Through the process of inner reflection on empirical data, the mind can discover and know the truth about the world. Descartes began by doubting everything. He ended with the conclusion that the only thing he couldn't doubt was that there was a

self that was doubting: *cogito ergo sum,* "I think, therefore I am." He could
have said, "I doubt, therefore I am." Descartes then sought to build all the
rest of knowledge, including knowledge about God, on this foundation of
reason (and skepticism).

This new approach to knowing drove the scientific revolution and gave
birth to a powerful new cultural vision that has guided the West through
four centuries of technological progress. The final end of the dominance of
the medieval Judeo-Christian worldview came at the halfway point, with
the theory of evolution and the application of Charles Darwin's (1809-
1882) work to a modern vision of a world that was understandable without
God. Earlier the astronomer Nicolaus Copernicus (1473-1543) had discovered that the earth revolved around the sun. The world was no longer at the
center of the universe. Now, with the work of the naturalist Darwin,
humans were no longer the crown of creation. Rather, they were the product of an eons-long process of random variation and natural selection, surviving only by the accidental development of consciousness. Consciousness
made humans the most fit of the animals to survive. Consciousness was
merely an accident, a byproduct of time, chance and struggle. What a long
way human beings had fallen from their perch at the top of the created
order, made in the image of God, inhabiting a paradise of harmony and
fruitfulness!

Yet, for moderns, what a long way humans had come. Man had come of
age, throwing off his psychological dependency on an omnipotent Parent in
the sky, emerging from the womb of the world to control his destiny and
exploit nature to his own benefit.

The Creator had become merely a divine architect, a master mathematician and clockmaker, while the universe was viewed as a uniformly regulated and fundamentally impersonal phenomenon, running on its own
perfect, immutable, mathematical laws. People had penetrated the universe's essential order and could now use that knowledge for their own
benefit and empowerment.

Truth was scientific, the self was autonomous and capable of understanding and controlling the physical world, and truth was discovered
through this rational, analytical mind.

So what were the questions people had about faith? People asked about
evidence for faith, proof of God's existence, logical arguments for God's
involvement in the world. Logical, scientific, analytical approaches to the

questions people were asking were very effective in speaking to a modern mindset. Today this approach still works with people who retain a modern mindset—for instance, some engineers. But many today see truth and how we know truth in a very different way.

The Ship Goes Down, the Heart Goes On

The movie *Titanic* provides striking images of this shift in cultural vision. The ship represents all that the modern has made possible. People have unlocked the secrets of nature and the world and created a ship that stands as a monument to their creative imagination and their technological and economic capacity to triumph. But what all these moderns don't realize is that they are trapped on a ship that is doomed to sink under its own weight.

The larger story is mirrored in the personal story of Rose. She is engaged to marry a great modern capitalist who controls the world through aggressive, visionary application of his reason and power. He is the lord of his world, and he protects his rank and privilege with all his power. Understandably, Rose is not happy. She is trapped, screaming out, suffocated by this world of power and privilege and lordly men.

Jack Dawson, the artist, the man who lives for the moment, the man who creates his own meaning and morality—his own reality—saves Rose in "every way a person can be saved." In gripping and visually captivating drama, the ship of modernism goes down. But in the end, all that death and destruction doesn't matter. What really matters is that the heart will go on (as expressed in the movie's theme song). And so the new cultural vision, the vision of the creative artist who makes reality and lives in a world of emotional truth and relational connection, is born and baptized and even triumphs. In a poignant moment, after telling the story of the Titanic, Rose staggers to the rail of another ship and throws the most valuable diamond in the world into the sea as a tribute to the man who led her into the new postmodern world and who died saving her decades earlier.

Transformation of Truth

Three dimensions of the postmodern mindset have particular impact on the questions people are asking and how we respond.

First, the idea of truth has been transformed. In medieval culture, truth was religious and universal. In modern culture, truth was scientific and universal. In a postmodern world, truth is experiential and personal or communal. People aren't looking for absolutes or universal truth. People today are looking for truth that is real, truth that resonates with their lives, their experiences and the experiences of their community.

Some people say postmoderns don't care about truth, they only have personal preferences. I don't agree. I think people influenced by postmodern culture are just as concerned about truth as people in the past. But postmodern people understand truth as local, personal, communal, experiential. They want to know what is true to life, their life.

On the downside of this transformation, defining universal values has become very difficult in our culture. Since there is no absolute truth, there are no universal values. But there are also good dimensions of this transformation in the way people understand truth. People today are less prone to false polarizations of head and heart and hand, thought and feeling and behavior. They can have a more integrated view of truth and reality, like that of the writers of the Bible. The Ten Commandments were the first doctrinal statement of the Hebrews. Head, heart and hand were integrated. Postmodern people long for that kind of authentic integration. Truth as philosophical or conceptual, truth divorced from feeling and action, is meaningless to postmodern people.

Therefore people are looking for communities in which faith is lived out and spiritual experiences are tangible and real. We answer people's questions when our lives and our words and our feelings all line up. People are hungry for such authenticity. People are hungry for genuine experiences of community and of God. Genuine worship is especially helpful in evangelism today because it can be an authentic experience of the reality of God in community. Healing experiences are also becoming more and more important for pre-Christian people.

This integrative approach can also help us answer the questions people have today.

Recently a friend asked me, "Don't all religions lead to the same place? Aren't we all just seeing the same ultimate reality from a different point of view?" Here's how I answered her:

Well, there are some pretty big differences among the various religions. They radically disagree about what God is like, and what you think God is like will affect deeply how you live. Mother Teresa is a good example of this. When she saw the poor and dying in Calcutta, she had to do something. She believed in a God who cares about the poor. Jesus spent most of his life healing and teaching and caring for the poor. So Mother Teresa's view of God led her to start a shelter in the shadow of a Hindu temple. She then took in the dying to comfort and love them in their last hours. She embraced those who were considered untouchable by most Hindus. Her commitment to a compassionate God who loves the poor led her to a very different response from that of the Hindus, who saw justice in the suffering of the poor and remained aloof.

You might be surprised to hear some of the other differences. Christian faith teaches that all people are created in God's image. That means all people are equal before God. Jesus lived out that teaching in the ways he treated the poor, women and social outcasts. Jesus believed all people matter to God. That's why Christians ran the Underground Railroad before the Civil War and why new Christian movements have often been led by women. That's why a person like Mother Teresa could do what she did in India, cradling and loving the dying, when most of her countrymen could not have brought themselves to touch the dying.

Notice, my answer focused on the behavioral and ethical impact of different beliefs. I didn't try to convince my friend that the different beliefs are logically inconsistent. "So what?" she would have responded. Instead I tried to convince her that different beliefs lead to radically different ways to live. She was very interested in that idea.

Today we need a personal, experiential approach to answering questions and defending our faith that is informed by good philosophy and good evidence. But we must start with personal experience.

When people ask me how God can be good and yet allow suffering, they are usually asking why God allowed something bad to happen to them. It's personal for them.

It needs to be personal for us too. When people tell me there are many ways to God, I first share some of the ways I tried to find God and how bankrupt those ways were for me. I tell people how messed up I am and how much I need what God did in Jesus. And then I ask them if they think they can do it on their own. If I know them well enough, I can challenge their assertions of self-righteousness. "No way!" I'll say, "You're almost as messed up as I am, and you need God's help!"

The Self in Community
A second transformation from the modern to postmodern mindset has to

do with the understanding of the self and of identity. The modern thinker saw the self as autonomous, individualistic and rational. The self was developed through analysis, discovery and self-expression. For instance, psychologist Erik Erikson posited that a person needs to achieve identity first and then is ready for intimacy. Psychologists today, such as Carol Gilligan, see identity and intimacy as inseparably connected. We construct our identity and our sense of self in community and through relationships and dialogue.

Consistent with Gilligan's theory, people are looking first for a community to belong to rather than a message to believe in. They are looking for a safe place to work out their sense of identity and self.

Rachel has a heart for her gay and lesbian friends and for her feminist friends. She met Jana through a Christian student in an InterVarsity group. Jana was certainly hostile to Christians. She peppered Rachel with questions about the failure of the church to affirm women and their giftedness. She denounced the Bible as a patriarchal book that had been used to oppress women for centuries. She couldn't relate to God as Father and didn't want to relate to Jesus as a man. She had grown up in a somewhat abusive home. And she hated it that Christians rejected the lesbian identity and lifestyle.

Rachel resisted the temptation to argue with Jana. Actually, Rachel wondered about some of the same things. And she told Jana that she wondered about them. Then she made an unusual challenge to Jana: "You know, I agree with you about so many things. Can we look at the biography of Jesus and see what Jesus has to say about some of these issues? Is he different? I would love to look at these biographies with you, because you'll help me see things I never saw before. Would you be willing to do that?"

Jana said, "Sure. I'll give it a try."

Rachel didn't pretend she had the answers Jana needed. She expressed a desire to learn from Jana. The arrogant benevolence of many approaches to witness was completely absent. And Rachel didn't pretend to have rationalizations for how the church and people in the Bible had treated women. She validated Jana's questions and even expressed that she had felt hurt by some of the same things.

In the past, being an expert and having the answers were what built credibility and a hearing. Today, having the same questions, struggles and hurts is what builds credibility and gains a hearing.

Rachel suggested they meet on a neutral turf, in the student union. This helped Jana feel in control.

Chapter seven offers a lot of help for leading this kind of study. At this point, suffice it to say, Jana was intrigued by the picture of Jesus she discovered as she and Rachel looked at stories of Jesus' interaction with others.

One of the questions Rachel asked toward the end of each discussion was what application Jesus' teaching might have on her own life and Jana's over the next week. Rachel encouraged Jana to try to put something Jesus talked about into practice. It was amazing to see the impact on both of them! It allowed Jesus' life to be relevant each week. It assumed that Jana would want to live wisely even if she hadn't yet decided to follow Jesus.

Today, people often come to Jesus by first trying to live by his wisdom and follow his lifestyle.

Each week Jana would try to bring the discussion back to the issue of women and how women have been treated in the church. Each week Rachel resisted being drawn into justifying past mistakes and sins of the church. She would empathize and then just keep bringing the focus gently back to Jesus.

Eight weeks in, Jana was obviously struggling. Rachel observed aloud, "Jesus is getting under your skin, isn't he?"

Jana responded, "Yes."

Rachel risked a comment. "You're really beginning to fall in love with Jesus, aren't you?"

Jana admitted she was. "But I can't! There are things in my life I don't want to give up!"

"Do you want me to share how I chose to trust in Jesus and began to work out my questions out of a relationship with God?" Rachel offered. "It won't answer all your questions, but Jesus will walk with you through your questions. I think you're ready for that."

Jana soon chose to put her life in the hands of God and ask Jesus to be at the center of her life. Her theology wasn't all worked out. But she knew she wanted to love, follow and trust Jesus.

People today are looking for a safe and accepting community in which to work out their identity. Jana had experienced rejection from Christians regarding her sense of self and identity. But because Rachel expressed the same concerns and had experienced the same hurts, she became a safe and accepting person with whom Jana could begin to work out her sense of self and identity. Rachel didn't start by confronting Jana's un-Christian ways of defining her identity. She started with accepting Jana's questions, identifying with her struggles and going with her to Jesus to work out her questions of identity along the way.

Ultimately we have to help people face God's view of their identity, personhood and sexuality. But we don't start there. We start where Jesus started. We start with Jesus, and with the offer of acceptance and a safe community in which to work out our identity and sense of self.

A Battle for the Imagination

Third, a transformation has taken place in the way people become convinced about moral and spiritual choices. In modernity, people were convinced by compelling, rational, logical arguments. In a postmodern world, the battle for allegiance is a battle for the spiritual and moral imagination of people. The arts have become the key arena for moral and spiritual discussion and exploration in our world.

Willie Jennings, a professor at Duke Divinity School, makes this point in a compelling way.

> How do we do our work of creating a compelling moral and spiritual vision in our day? There is now an immense interest in the university in art and its relation to truth, goodness and beauty. There is a growing commitment to art as the primary way for re-making the moral and spiritual imagination. The arts are becoming the arena in which moral vision is being made and re-made. The arts create moral value. If you want to capture the moral and spiritual imagination, you invite in the poets and musicians. Intellectuals who align themselves with pop culture are being listened to at the university. (Jennings, 2000)

One way to sum up the modern mindset is that it is the attempt to empirically and rationally know, control and engineer reality. This is the work of the scientist.

One way to sum up the postmodern mindset is that it is the attempt to insightfully perceive, imagine and create reality. This is the work of the artist.

Interestingly, in a postmodern world the differences between the scientist and the artist are blurring, coming together. Science is more and more about the imagination, and art is more and more about technology. The two approaches are becoming integrated in the ways we think, imagine, feel and make commitments.

We imagine and create our own identity in community.

We imagine and create our own computer-generated world of information and virtual reality.

Even in the world of science we are beginning to create our own reality through recombinant DNA technologies and cloning. Human beings are becoming masters of biological processes and are beginning to re-create humanity.

And of course we create our own spiritual reality through the imaginative and regenerative powers of the soul.

Image has ascended over word. The screen is in ascendance over the printed page.

Thus the ancient traditions of liturgy and sacrament and mystery are now returning to center stage in our efforts to reach this generation. There is a longing for image that has the power to point to the transcendent. The spiritual and moral imagination can be captured by this kind of ancient-future faith (see Robert Webber's book by that title).

The uses of media and movies for communicating and exploring truth have exploded. Our evangelism must take this revolution into account.

How does this affect the ways we respond to people's questions today? We must become great storytellers, verbally and through media. We want not only to respond to the questions logically but to capture people's spiritual and moral imagination. For instance, we can use Morpheus from *The Matrix* as an image of a mentor who sets us free by the truth. We can tell stories, using images as well as words, of churches ministering to people with AIDS, adopting unwanted children, feeding the poor and hungry, and addressing environmental problems. These stories can capture the imagination and convince people that faith can make a difference!

Looking Ahead

Evangelism that takes account of these three key transformations will be explored in the rest of the book.

First, people today are looking for truth that is experiential, for communities in which faith is lived out and for spiritual experiences that are tangible and real. *So experience comes before explanation.*

Second, people today are looking for a safe and accepting community in which to work out their identity. *So belonging comes before believing.*

Third, the battle for allegiance today is a battle for people's spiritual and moral imagination. *So image comes before word.*

As we understand these changes and needs, we can learn to respond to people's questions in much more compelling ways. The next chapter will explore a theological basis and strategy for reaching people today in a way that best serves their process of coming home to God.

Discussion Questions

1. Do you agree that people today are looking for truth that is experiential, for communities in which faith is lived out, and for spiritual experiences that are tangible and real? How might that change the way you and your ministry view and do evangelism? Look back at the way I responded to my friend who wondered if Christ was the only way. How would you respond to that question? Did you learn anything that would help you respond to your friends?

2. Do you agree that people today are looking for a safe and accepting community in which to work out their identity? How might that change the way you and your ministry view and do evangelism? Look back at the way Rachel reached Jana. What did you notice and learn from her story that could help you reach people like Jana?

3. Do you agree that the battle for allegiance today is a battle for the spiritual and moral imagination of people? How might that change the way you and your ministry view and do evangelism? What's one movie you could use to discuss truth with your friends and to help capture their moral and spiritual imagination?

4. What's one step you want to take with your pre-Christian friends in light of these changes?

4

A THEOLOGY & STRATEGY FOR REACHING PEOPLE TODAY

JOHN WESLEY LIVED IN ENGLAND IN THE EIGHTEENTH CENTURY AND WAS greatly used of God to reach his world for Christ. Unchurched members of the working classes were especially responsive to his ministry.

Much in Wesley's approach was aimed at a Christian culture. And yet Wesley had his greatest impact among the unchurched and pagan masses. Wesley's process of conversion and order of salvation fit the pagan culture of his day. And with George Hunter at Asbury Seminary and others, I suggest that Wesley's process and order of salvation are a great fit for today's experiential, community seeking person. Wesley's process can be adapted well to the way postmodern people today think, feel, imagine and commit.

Wesley's way of expressing and practicing faith has also had a great impact in many nonwhite cultures around the world. The Holiness, Pentecostal and charismatic movements, which have been successful in Black, Korean and Latino cultures, all have strong roots in Wesley's approach to

Christian faith and witness. As we think about how to reach people in a very diverse world who are looking for a safe place to work out their sense of identity and self, Wesley's insights can be quite helpful.

Four Steps into God's Kingdom

Wesley had a four-step vision and practice for his order or process of salvation. I am deeply indebted to Hunter for the theological insights that follow. He is free from blame for any of the ways I stretch and apply his insights!

First, people were *awakened*. Wesley went to where the people were. He preached in the open air, where he could get a hearing among the common people, much to the chagrin and then criticism of people in the church. "How uncouth!" they said. "How culturally low!" What a caving in to the culture of his day, especially the low culture, the culture of the barroom and coal mine. Educated Christians had written the common people off as unreachable, uninterested, ignorant and spiritually closed. Wesley preached to thousands of workers who rarely darkened the door of a church. He preached to awaken them to their lostness, their sins and their need for grace. I call this stage *soul awakening* to make it more descriptive for us today.

Second, an awakened seeker was *welcomed* into the fellowship of a Methodist class meeting. Here members shared their struggles and sins and prayed and rooted for each other to live better lives. After a few months, the seeker joined the larger Methodist Society, whether she had become a believer or not. I will call this stage of being welcomed *community*.

Wesley believed that "belonging comes before believing." Evangelism is about helping people belong so that they can believe (Hunter, p. 29). Wesley believed that gathering Christians and pre-Christians together to confess their sins and encourage one another was key to the release of the church's contagious compassion, powerful faith and daring apostolic courage (Hunter, p. 21). And apparently he was right for the church in his day!

Third, the class meeting leader taught the pre-Christian to experience *justification*, God's acceptance and the gifts of faith and new life. The class leader encouraged people not just to sign a doctrinal statement or pray a simple prayer but to seek God until they received assurance of their salvation. Wesley wanted to see a faith that connected to people's hearts as well as to their heads and that followed a commitment of their whole will to seek God until he might be found. I will call this stage *conversion*, because this word is more understood in Christian and non-Christian circles today.

Fourth, the class leader taught people to expect to experience *sanctification*, even to the point of becoming free from sin's power. This teaching of Wesley was certainly controversial. But he had seen so much religion without power that he called people to faith in a God who transforms our lives. If there is no transformation, was there genuine faith to begin with? Thus I will call this stage *transformation*.

Soul Awakening. Community. Conversion. Transformation. Here is an order and process of salvation that can help us understand and focus on the steps by which people today can be led to genuine faith in Christ.

Today's pre-Christian person may be spiritually curious. Spiritual curiosity is high, especially in "create your own" spiritualities. But people in a postmodern world need their soul *awakened* to the depth and power of their spiritual longings, and they need to begin to connect to Jesus as a potential satisfier of their spiritual hunger. I believe effective soul-awakening events and efforts are the weakest link in our attempts to reach people in today's world.

Today people are certainly looking for a *community* to belong to before a message to believe in. So we desperately need communities that welcome the awakened seeker. Our communities, like those of Wesley's day, aren't attractive to most pre-Christian people. I believe drawing pre-Christian people into attractive communities is the heart and soul of reaching people today.

Today people need to hear a message that connects to the heart as well as the head and that works to make life better, to turn life around. Our good news must make sense and lead people into the truths of *conversion* and the experience of it. It must speak to people's deepest hunger for identity and a sense of self.

People must also see that faith makes a difference. Our good news must result in not just a prayer that is prayed or a doctrine that is affirmed but a life that is turned upside down and changed from the inside out. People must cultivate their true identity in Christ. That is *transformation* for a postmodern new believer.

Prior to all these steps, people today are intensely relational and distrustful. They will not usually respond to a stranger at a big event. They need to be befriended and loved and accepted before they will check out our soul-awakening events or visit our community.

I summarize this process for pre-Christians at the end of this chapter, as a strategy for reaching people today.

The Celtic Way

Perhaps surprisingly, another helpful pattern for reaching people in a post-modern world with the gospel comes from the early Celtic Christians—and here too George Hunter has done valuable work. (Hunter's investigation of "the Celtic way of mission" is summarized in "The 'Celtic' Way for Evangelizing Today," *The Journal of the Academy for Evangelism in Theological Education,* 1997-1998, pp. 15-30.) Celtic culture and the Celtic way of mission can be profoundly instructive. This way of mission was much more affirming of indigenous cultures than the more dominant Roman way, which bundled Roman religion with Roman culture. The Celtic paradigm of evangelism and mission illustrates well many of the changes that we need to make in our theology and practice. Hunter looks at the life of St. Patrick in his development of the Celtic model.

Patrick, the patron saint of Ireland, spent eight years in slavery under Celtic lords, learning the culture and language of the Irish people. He learned to pray without ceasing and became devout. Directed in a dream, Patrick set out toward the coast, found a ship waiting and sailed in freedom to Rome, where he obtained a theological education. At age forty-eight, while serving as a parish priest in England, he had another dream in which faces of those he remembered in Ireland called to him to bring the gospel. The Vatican validated his "Macedonian call," ordained him a bishop and sent him to reach some of the 150 unreached Celtic tribes in Ireland. By the time of his death, St. Patrick had reached fifteen to twenty of these tribes and set the pattern for the work of Columba, Brigid, Columbanus, Aiden and many others in reaching pagan tribes all over Europe. Aiden's missionary effort is retold in novel form by Stephen Lawhead in *Byzantium.* Many of the distinctives of this Celtic way of evangelism and mission are fleshed out in that novel.

Hunter points out these distinctives; I have added to, paraphrased, summarized and shortened his discussion for the purpose of this book.

1. *Nature.* While Roman Christianity emphasized humanity's differences from and dominion over nature, the Celtic movement stressed humanity's kinship with nature. We are in the middle of a renaissance in concern for

nature and the environment. Our way of mission must speak to humanity's relations with nature in a new way.

2. *Human nature.* While Augustine saw human nature as depraved, Celtic Christians believed sin had blurred and twisted but not bent beyond recognition the image of God in human beings. Therefore Celtic missionaries left room for honoring the achievements of people who had no conscious relationship with God. Postmodern people will not even listen to us if we write off all that is good and glorious in the achievements of men and women, Christian or not, culturally and scientifically.

3. *God's presence.* While Roman Christianity emphasized God's transcendence, Celtic Christians emphasized God's immanence. The hymn/prayer "St. Patrick's Breastplate" is a good example of this focus:

> Christ be with me, Christ within me,
> Christ behind me, Christ before me,
> Christ beside me, Christ to win me,
> Christ to comfort and restore me,
> Christ beneath me, Christ above me,
> Christ in quiet, Christ in danger,
> Christ in hearts of all that love me,
> Christ in mouth of friend and stranger.

Postmoderns long for an immediate presence in their lives. They long for a God who knows them, loves them and gets involved in the daily stuff of their lives in a way that makes a practical difference. They long for a God who knows their name and can bless and call forth their truest identity.

4. *God's power.* While Roman Christianity emphasized God's stability and order, Celtic Christians emphasized God's dynamic activity. God was powerfully at work to heal and to triumph over every other source of life and object of worship. Often in pagan cultures, the power encounter between God and other gods was a decisive moment in the conversion of a people. Similarly, postmoderns often report experiencing God's presence and seeing God's power at work in their lives as the key moment in their turn toward God.

5. *Organization.* Where Roman Christians emphasized preserving their institutions and traditions, Celtic Christians emphasized advancing as a movement through community. Although the Celts had parish churches and priests, the monasteries or abbeys were much more central to Celtic

Christianity. They were the busiest institutions in Celtic society, filled with people and fulfilling the roles of school, library, hospital, guest house, arts center and mission station. Their organization was significantly "flatter" than the Roman pattern. Women were as likely to be the chief leaders, and people were addressed by name or as "brother" or "sister" more often than by title. Mission was done in teams or bands, in community. Celtic historian Peter Tremayne's mystery book *Absolution by Murder* presents good examples of the role women had in Celtic culture. Sister Fidelma, the heroine, would be a great role model for many women today.

Postmoderns aren't concerned about organizational hierarchy. They want to see people honored and free to use their gifts and abilities regardless of culture and gender. This organic approach to organization leads to community that today's postmodern is very attracted to.

6. *Culture*. Where Roman Christians assumed Roman culture was superior to all other cultures, Celtic Christians worked indigenously and contextually. They adapted to each culture well, and so their movement spread very rapidly.

This emphasis gets at some of the heart of the goal of this book. God's handprints are all over our own culture. People's spiritual interest is high. The culture lies under God's judgment, and we can never forget that fact. But the culture is full of opportunity, if we can just receive from God the eyes to see the spiritual need around us. Billy Graham has traveled all over the world and has found spiritual hunger everywhere. He has always been able to identify cultural expressions of that hunger that he can affirm and use to stimulate interest in the gospel.

Some Christians look at our culture and see only disintegration and death ahead. They have the eyes of the prophet. We need prophets. But oh, how we need evangelists who love postmodern people enough to see postmodern culture with new eyes and a new heart!

7. *Religion*. Where Roman Christians treated other religions as irrelevant or demonic, Celtic Christians saw the religion of pagans as evidence of spiritual interest and a preparation for the gospel. Pagan practices and symbols, like the standing stones, the sacred groves and springs, the power of circle, the poems, runes and chants, were baptized into Christian faith wherever possible. For the Celts, Jesus was the fulfillment of pagan religion more than the destroyer of pagan religion.

Frank Peretti's books were extremely popular with Christians a few years back. Peretti was a good representative of the Roman tradition: in his novels all spiritual expressions of a postmodern consciousness seemed to be part of a worldwide demonic conspiracy. *Star Wars* gets lumped into that conspiracy in his second book, *Piercing the Darkness*. And yet as we'll see in the next chapter, *Star Wars* can be a profoundly helpful picture of the nature of spiritual interest today and a very useful bridge for us. Is the postmodern culture's spiritual ethos demonic? Or is it a sign pointing to the inescapable spiritual hunger of every human being? Could it be both? Might God want both prophets and evangelists? Might God want them to cooperate and collaborate and understand their own strengths and limitations?

8. *Communication*. Where Roman Christians emphasized a "left-brained," rational, propositional, didactic, doctrinal exposition model for communicating the faith, Celtic Christians took a more "right-brained," imaginative approach. The Romans taught the content of the faith. The Celts helped people discover the meaning of the faith, through visual images like the Celtic knot and the Celtic cross, through art, drama, music, story, analogy and poetry. They worked more to evoke and experience truth than to explain truth. A good example to teach the Trinity:

> Three folds of the cloth, yet only one napkin is there,
> Three joints of the finger, but still only one finger fair;
> Three leaves of the shamrock, yet no more than one shamrock to wear,
> Frost, snow-flakes and ice, all in water their origin share,
> Three Persons in God; to one God alone we make prayer. (Hunter, p. 25)

The imagination and intuition as ways of knowing are seeing tremendous resurgence. The rational mind's ability to stand alone has been exhausted. The imagination is a fountain of renewal to the life of the mind in our day. Jesus' way of teaching truth, in stories and symbols, is once again coming back into its own. Our imaginative communication, our use of the arts, our speaking in story, myth and fable are now the very language of the heart to reach a postmodern world.

9. *Mission*. Roman Christians preached, called for a decision, and then began churches when people believed. Celtic Christians, in contrast, invited people into their monastic communities to belong before they believed. Celtic monasteries were colonies of laypeople devoted to prayer, discipline, practical love, evangelism and hospitality. Religious brothers and sisters went out in teams to befriend pre-Christian people, to serve and

communicate Christian faith through conversation, analogies and stories. They invited responsive people to spend time in their communities to experience fellowship, worship and service and to ask questions and explore faith. Wandering missionary bands set up communities of prayer, contemplation and service, and if their mission bore fruit, a new monastery or abbey would be born.

Such loving, serving, listening and open community is at the heart of effective mission to a postmodern world. The following chapters will help us see how. They follow Wesley's order of salvation, and they weave in the insights of the Celtic way of mission, so powerful for reaching pagan cultures in the medieval ages and, I suggest, as powerful for reaching postmodern pagans today.

*   *   *   *

A Strategy for Reaching Postmoderns (adapted from John Wesley)

Pre-Christians today go through a process. They are befriended, accepted, loved. Their soul is then awakened to its existence, to its spiritual hunger and to the possibility of Jesus. They join an attractive community to experience love and to explore and experience God. The gospel addresses their hurt and their sin and their longing for identity and a sense of self, and they convert. The Spirit then begins to transform them from the inside out. So here is a simple strategy to reach people today.

☐ **Build** *friendships* **and pray.** Nothing is more important, but this cannot stand alone!

☐ **Hold** *soul-awakening* **events.** We need to create contexts for the Holy Spirit to awaken people to their spiritual longings and begin to see Jesus as a possible satisfier of those longings. This step may be the biggest missing link in our evangelism strategy.

☐ **Draw pre-Christians into seeking** *community.* Postmodern people are looking for a community to belong to before a message to believe in. This step is the centerpiece for reaching people today.

☐ **Challenge pre-Christians to** *conversion.* Where and when and how do you challenge people to become Christians?

☐ **Help new Christians into** *transformation.* Changed lives are our greatest apologetic for the gospel.

*   *   *   *

Discussion Questions

1. Think about how you came to know Christ. What was your process? How does it fit with Wesley's order of salvation? Are there elements of the Celtic way of missions and evangelism that were especially helpful in your own process?

2. Think of your friends that you are praying for and trying to reach. What stage are they at in the process that Wesley suggested? What is their next step? How could you help?

3. What elements of the Celtic way of mission would be most helpful to your friends? How could you and your ministry grow in those elements?

4. Look over the next page, a strategy for reaching postmodern people. What are your responses to this strategy? Where is your ministry or church strong, and where are you weak, in light of this suggested strategy?

5

THE POWER
OF TEAM

Before we explore more fully this strategy for reaching people today, we need to think about teamwork. I believe teamwork is the essential foundation and presupposition for pursuing any evangelism strategy effectively in our day.

Frustration, Motivation and Team
I had worked at Exxon Research and Engineering Company for four months. I had struggled spiritually. I was just barely beginning to feel connected to my new church. I felt overwhelmed with work. I had made new friends slowly. I don't think I had shared my faith even once.

I was ready to conclude that evangelism just wasn't for me. I felt introverted. I didn't have much to say. No one would be interested. My life just wasn't that hot. Who would want to become like me?

Then I began to experience some spiritual renewal through a special speaker our pastor brought in. And four of us at Exxon began meeting as a small group once a week. We began to pray for each other and for other coworkers at Exxon. We began to talk about people and what we could do to reach out and who had what gifts to help in reaching out.

That next week, energized by community and a sense of team, I had conversations with nine different people about my faith! Now I felt evangelism was the thing to do. Of course evangelism was for me. What else would I be doing?

The small group started praying harder. We decided to go on a ski trip and invite our pre-Christian friends. Several came. It was amazing to see us work together. Sue had a gift of hospitality. She helped us plan the trip and take care of food and fun. Carol had a gift of mercy. She was deeply sensitive to how people were feeling and got into several conversations about the pain in their lives. Art had a gift for prayer; sometimes he wiped out on the slopes because his mind was engaged in asking God to work. And I had a gift of gab. I ended up in significant conversation about spiritual things, especially with two of our friends. As we continued to build friendships after the ski trip, Mike eventually responded to Christ.

Who led Mike to Christ?

We all did, collaborating with God. Every one of our gifts was crucial. We were each a critical link in the chain. We were community to each other and a team together in witness.

I was shocked at the impact of that team in my life. I turned from evangelistic mouse to powerhouse in a week, just because of the encouragement and spiritual nurture of that group of people.

One summer I went to Ireland with Operation Mobilization, a radical missions organization. It was a very important and stretching experience for me. But I almost resigned as an evangelist during that summer.

Here's what happened. We started in Dublin with a van, twenty boxes of books and eight shillings. We drove to Thurles, in County Tipperary, southern Ireland. A believer there graciously gave us his home for the summer. Our team of eight woke up the first morning at the insistence of our German team leader. It was 6:00 a.m., time for calisthenics! After calisthenics we asked Matthias what the plan for the day was.

"We're going to go door to door, share our faith and sell good Christian literature. Whatever we make, we will use to buy our food with."

I groaned a little, though not so Matthias could hear me. I hated the idea of knocking on doors of strangers. But I went. After a hard beginning, I actually saw God do some good things. I reached the end of the day thankful and rejoicing but also looking forward to other ways of reaching out.

After calisthenics on Wednesday, the next day, we asked with bated breath about the plans for the day.

"We're going to go door to door, share our faith and sell good Christian literature. Whatever we make, we will use to buy our food with."

That sounded kind of familiar to me. Obediently I did it, saw God work again, but went to bed tired, anxious for a new plan!

Next morning: "We're going to go door to door, share our faith and sell good Christian literature. Whatever we make, we will use to buy our food with."

Then on Saturday, Matthias surprised us: "We're going to do something new, something really different and special. We're going to go downtown, set up a small podium and preach to the passersby. Isn't that exciting? Rick, you'll preach first."

Yeehaw! I couldn't wait. That is, I couldn't wait until I woke up from this impending nightmare!

That was Saturday. The next Monday, Matthias let us know we would be back going door to door. But he needed a volunteer to shop and do laundry. My hand shot up faster than the speed of light! I had no idea that I had such passion for shopping and laundry. But at that moment, I was sure my spiritual gifts went more in that direction than toward evangelism.

In the end, the summer was immensely valuable, a kind of Christian boot camp in risk-taking that I will remember forever. But I decided several times that summer that evangelism was probably not my gift, because I hated going door to door and talking with strangers. *I just must not have gifts in evangelism,* I concluded.

Since then, my attitude has changed. Today I am helping lead evangelism nationally for InterVarsity Christian Fellowship, a campus ministry on seven hundred campuses in the country and with sister movements in 120 countries in the world. What changed my attitude toward and involvement in evangelism?

My friend Mark Mittleburg at the Willow Creek Association had a similar experience in England. He decided evangelism wasn't for him, because he too disliked confrontational evangelism. But a year or so later, he became evangelism director for the largest and possibly most evangelistic church in the United States.

What changed for him?

The key for us both is that we began thinking of evangelism as a team effort. In a team, each of us has a different temperament and different gifts. Each of us can play a different role in an overall evangelism strategy. As we became involved in witness in and through team ministry, we found that we had a very important place in pre-Christians' process of coming to know and love Jesus. You can find that true in your life too.

Styles of Evangelism

One helpful approach to discovering your place on God's team to reach postmodern people is the "Styles of Evangelists" tool developed by Mark and others at Willow Creek Community Church. This test can be obtained through the "Becoming a Contagious Christian" course in relational evangelism.

The styles identified by this course include

1. confrontational
2. intellectual
3. testimonial
4. interpersonal
5. invitational
6. serving

Scriptural examples of each style are also given.

At Exxon, Sue was interpersonal and testimonial. Carol was serving and invitational. I was intellectual and a bit confrontational, though not the door-to-door and open-air type of confrontational! Art practiced a seventh style, a prayer style of evangelism. We were a great evangelism team—and God used us!

When you think about reaching your neighborhood or workplace or dorm floor or university department for Christ, you may feel overwhelmed, inadequate, paralyzed. You and I need a team! We need a team to reach our neighborhood. We need a team to reach our workplace. We need a team to reach our postmodern friends.

Postmodern people understand the importance of community. They understand the place of teams in the workplace.

We need to learn from this great postmodern (and biblical!) insight. We need community. We need team. Witness will thrive as we work together in teams.

That is true for us as individuals. It will also be true for us as churches and ministries. As we pursue a simple strategy for reaching postmodern people, we will best bear fruit in and through teams.

So let's look at teamwork in relation to our basic strategy. What kinds of teams will reach postmodern people?

Build Friendships and Pray

Pray for God to raise up a partner or three to work with you in reaching your friends! There is a couple in our neighborhood with whom my wife and I have prayed and sponsored neighborhood gatherings. They were our team. Having a team kept us moving forward, praying together, feeding the fire of our hearts for reaching the people in our neighborhood. We hosted a neighborhood block party with them. We planned a neighborhood Christmas gathering with them. Through these events we learned who in our neighborhood were celebrating promotions and achievements, who were grieving because of divorce and kid problems.

Our teammates have just moved to Maryland. So we need a new team. I've been praying, and a Christian couple just moved in up the street. They seem ideal. Praise God! I think God loves to answer our prayers for team!

In addressing the next several steps of the strategy, I have been greatly helped by the ideas of Wayne Cordeiro, pastor of a six-thousand-member church in Hawaii. His church develops all its ministries through what he calls *fractal teams*. Fractal teams are teams that multiply, all having the same basic pattern.

Every ministry that is launched can be represented with a circle. Cordeiro divides the circle into quadrants and labels each quadrant. The circle represents the ministry or strategy being launched. Each quadrant represents a job that needs to be done to launch the strategy or ministry. He has every team leader answer the primary question of mission: what's the team for? Then the team leader is asked to divide the ministry into the four things that have to get done in order to fulfill that ministry. Then the leader recruits four more leaders, one for every task or part that must be done.

Hold Soul-Awakening Events

We will need a team to pull off good soul-awakening events. We will also need a good team leader. Four things need to happen to bring about good soul awakening events: prayer, program, publicity and follow-up. So we will need a good leader over each area. The program area could easily have its own team of four covering drama, music, media and technical issues.

As our soul-awakening events become more and more successful, we can develop more teams to take on different tasks. Every team member will then be part of reaching the people God has called us to reach.

Draw Pre-Christians into Seeking Community

I recruited a partner to work with me on my first seeker small group designed to help pre-Christians find community while exploring their questions concerning faith. It was important for us to make sure the pre-Christians outnumbered the Christians, once we started to focus on seekers. As my partner and I worked together, we encouraged one another and kept moving forward. When I didn't know how to help my pre-Christian friend ask Jesus to be his leader and forgiver, my Christian teammate did.

In the first chapter of this book I recounted my experience of working with a team of eight people at the University of Wisconsin-Madison to invite freshmen into small groups. I was astonished at the impact of working together. I will never forget the exuberance and boldness of Shelley. She was a quiet, introverted person. But in the context of team, she was a lioness! She recruited nearly ten people herself. God doesn't change our personality, but he can certainly give us more boldness and guts in taking risks when we work as part of a team.

We launched Alpha at our church through a team. Alpha is an evangelistic program that many churches have adopted. It started at an Anglican church in England. Each Alpha meeting has a meal, a short period of worship, a talk and a small group discussion time. We assigned one person to hospitality and food, one to small groups, one to music and testimonies, and one to recruiting speakers. Putting Alpha together was one of the most powerful, enjoyable and fruitful team experiences of my life.

Challenge Pre-Christians to Conversion

One great way pre-Christians are coming to know and love Jesus is through seeker retreats. Seeker retreats provide an experience of community and open the possibility of an encounter with God.

So get a leader and a team to pull together a retreat. I am preparing to speak at one of these even as I write. There will be two hundred students at a weekend event called True Love 2000. Fifty of them will be postmodern pre-Christians. I can't wait!

Help New Christians into Transformation

Develop prayer teams and prayer ministry. It is exciting to see the hunger for healing among postmodern people today. There is nothing quite like ministering healing in and through teams. A team of us once led ninety students from the University of Chicago into a time of healing and transformation as they faced painful issues of sexuality and experiences in broken families. You have to have a team to do that kind of ministry. Postmodern pre-Christians are often profoundly moved during times of prayer ministry.

At one event in a large urban church I was part of, the pastor invited people to come to the front for prayer. I had trained twenty people to pray in pairs (teams) for others. The pastor said in his invitation, "The worst thing that can happen to you is you will have an experience of being profoundly loved. That's not so bad, is it? And the best that can happen is that you might hear the voice of the Master, saying, 'Go in peace, my daughter, my son. Your faith has made you whole.'"

Our prayer teams were flooded with people hungry for that kind of touch, empathy and prayer. We had about thirty minutes of prayer for people, Christian and pre-Christian. What a team experience of seeing God work in a way we will never forget! Fifteen years later, that church continues to offer the same powerful and open invitation to prayer.

Where's Your Team?

Paul worked in and through teams. Jesus worked in and through a team of twelve, and a smaller team of three. On teams we find the encouragement and nurture we need to take risks in relationships. In teams we are able to collaborate with other people who need our gifts just as we need theirs. Through team we can see God bear more and better fruit among our postmodern friends. They will be as drawn by the quality of our community as by the excellence of our programs.

Where's your team? God give us hearts to pray, eyes to see and strength to commit ourselves to teams that can reach postmodern people.

Now let's pursue our simple strategy to reach people today. And let's keep the commitment to and value of team as a theme that weaves throughout our thinking about evangelism from here on.

Discussion Questions

1. What do you think your style of evangelism might be? Refer to the list of the different styles on page 65. What kinds of people with other styles might you need to work with in order to be effective?

2. Who might you be able to work with in evangelism? Who could be on your team?

3. Spend some time praying for God to raise up team members and teamwork in evangelism for you.

6

FRIENDSHIP & PRAYER

I HAVE BEEN A CHRISTIAN FOR TWENTY-FIVE YEARS NOW. THAT PUTS ME AT
high risk. I may be "hunkering in the bunker" (a graphic phrase from
Leonard Sweet's *Soul Tsunami*). I may be "happy in the holy huddle," "safe
in the sanctuary," "fond of the fortress." Bluntly put, I may not have many
pre-Christian friends. That's an all too common tragedy. We spend all our
weekends and evenings out with Christians. We are in small groups with
Christians. Our church basketball league is almost all Christians. We go to
events, or watch them on television, with Christian friends.

How sad, when Jesus has a much more exciting adventure for us. He
invites us to come with him to find the lost sheep. He promises to be with
us when we go into all the world. As we hunker in the bunker and look
around for Jesus, it turns out that he is up on the battlefield recruiting new
soldiers from the enemy! As we sit safe in the sanctuary looking around for
Jesus, he's out in the storm offering sanctuary to the blown and the tossed.

Now I realize that God is everywhere, and he is certainly present when
Christians are together in worship. I'm not out to be heretical. But God is

especially present in stretching and faith-building ways where his kingdom is being proclaimed and advanced.

I've always struggled with the parable of the lost sheep. Jesus leaves the ninety-nine to go find the one lost sheep. I see myself as one of the ninety-nine. Doesn't Jesus care about me?

Then one day I realized there was a way to address my dilemma. I could follow Jesus. If I went out looking for the lost sheep, he would never leave me or forsake me. Many of us have an impoverished experience of Jesus because we spend most of our time with the found. Jesus just isn't the hunker-in-the-bunker type.

Getting out of the Bunker

So several years ago I got serious about building new friendships with pre-Christian neighbors and associates. And I ran into some challenges. I'm a busy guy. Fellowship is important to me. I don't naturally overlap with pre-Christians in my work and social life.

Here are some things that helped me begin to get out there with Jesus.

First, I began to include pre-Christians in any activity I normally did with Christians.

The Superbowl was just around the corner. Usually my church small group watched it together, and that was our plan again. But I had been challenged in a relational evangelism course to include pre-Christians in my normal activities. What better opportunity than the Superbowl? I took it as a chance to get to know my neighbors better.

MaryKay and I invited fifteen folks from the neighborhood. Ten came. My small group from church came too. Even though my team (the Green Bay Packers) lost, it was the most fun I have ever had watching a Superbowl.

Second, I began "strategic consumerism" (a concept described in the Becoming a Contagious Christian course). I am writing this book at Einstein Bagels, where I am reaching out to the staff. I am building relationships with them. Just yesterday I found a Christian employee there. I have found my teammate! He and I are beginning to talk about reaching the other people who work at Einstein. The worker at the Borders Café knows me well too.

Third, I am choosing to pursue interests that put me in the world of pre-Christians. I need exercise. I am exercising and reaching out at the health club. I love skiing and fly-fishing and am finding ways to do those things with lost people. I am deeply interested in my kids. So are most parents! I have used coaching my kids as a way to build friendships with pre-Christians.

Churches and ministries can have a great impact by sponsoring bridge events, events that help their members develop friendships with pre-Christian people: movie nights, healthy party nights, Taste of Chicago (or whatever community you are from) nights, other fun and frolicking ways to enjoy life and build those friendships. A church in southern California recently drew thirty-eight thousand people for a gala Labor Day celebration. Luis Palau, a well-known Latin American evangelist who now lives in Portland, Oregon, has pioneered a massive summer festival in his community. What great ways to have fun and build friends! It can also be extremely trust-building to ask for help from a pre-Christian friend. While pre-Christians are in the role of the giver, they are especially open to discussing experiences and convictions.

Jesus' Pattern

As I begin and pursue these friendships, I am practicing Jesus' pattern of relationship and witness in Matthew 9:35-39. Lon Allison of the Billy Graham Center has been very helpful to me here. He has suggested that Jesus practiced a three-step process of evangelism: prayer, care and share.

Jesus heard from the Father about where he was to go and whom he was to heal and to teach. He prayed that God would raise up other evangelists to reach people he couldn't. For Jesus, this was the *prayer* part of evangelism.

He didn't just pray, and he didn't just preach and teach. He heard and healed. He touched and transformed. For Jesus, there was a *care* part of evangelism. In his book *Conspiracy of Kindness* author Steve Sjogren offers many suggestions for practicing this care.

But Jesus didn't just love people and hope they got it. He preached and taught. He proclaimed the kingdom and explained what people were experiencing. Experience came before explanation. In that way Jesus was a true postmodern (only he was a *pre*!). But there was also always explanation and exclamation. For Jesus, this was the *share* part of evangelism. Jesus knew how to live out loud.

True friendship involves all three. We pray for our friends. And we pray *with* our friends.

We care for our friends, and we let them care for us.

We share with our friends, after we listen and before we listen again!

My brother Mike began to date a Christian woman in his senior year of high school. For several years I had been praying for Mike to come to know Christ. When I came home from college, I began praying my heart out for an opportunity to share with him. God had another priority. As I talked with Mike one day, he began to share with me what a hurtful older brother I had been. He remembered vividly the day I had pelted him with eggs, the day I lost my temper and swore and chased him around the house, the day I seemed uninterested in his struggles.

I committed myself to care for Mike. I listened better. I asked his forgiveness. I realized that family members rarely listen to words but are blown away by true caring.

I kept caring for him and praying for him. Finally, the summer before he went to college, he and I drove to the Outer Banks in North Carolina. We spent five hours in the car, just the two of us. Finally, I got to share. I shared how much God meant to me and how God had changed my life. I asked him if he had any barriers to committing himself to Christ. He did. I spent three hours answering tough questions. I thought that I had done well, that I had dunked the ball in the hoop in answering the questions. So I asked him if he was ready to give his life to God.

"Nope. I have to think about it. But you'll be the first to know," Mike promised.

"Can I pray for you, Mike?" I asked.

"Sure," he responded.

"Now?"

"OK," Mike said, a little less enthusiastically. But I did. And I felt God lead me in praying for Mike as he went off to school. God gave me insight. And Mike felt loved.

Then he headed off to Penn State. I was disappointed. But I kept praying. Then I got his first letter from campus. Can you imagine how it started? "Praise the Lord." Wow! I was excited. I read on. "I got to campus, and the first person I ran into on my dorm floor was a Christian who wondered if I wanted to give my life to God. At that point I said, 'I give up. If you want me this badly, God, then I'll give my life to you!' Praise the Lord, huh, Rick?"

Praise the Lord indeed!

Let's get unhunkered from the bunker and get into the world of pre-Christians, investing ourselves in relationship.

And let's follow Jesus' model of witness.

Prayer evangelism.

Care evangelism.

Share evangelism.

Evangelism like Jesus!

Evangelism *with* Jesus!

Discussion Questions

1. Are you mostly "hunkered in the bunker," spending your time with Christians, or are you out there with Jesus, building meaningful relationships with pre-Christian people? Look at the ideas that helped me build friendships. What might help you build stronger friendships?

2. How are you and your ministry or church doing in prayer evangelism? care evangelism? share evangelism? What next steps do you want to take?

3. What events could your ministry sponsor that would encourage those involved to build friendships with pre-Christians?

Many books have been written and programs developed on the kind of relational evangelism I write about in this chapter. Paul Little's *How to Give Away Your Faith*, Becky Pippert's *Out of the Saltshaker*, Mack Stiles's *Speaking of Jesus* and Mark Mittelberg's Becoming a Contagious Christian course are only a few. Therefore I've kept this chapter short and sweet. But read these great books and resources. This step is the foundation of all the other steps. That has always been true, but it is even more true in a postmodern world.

7

A BIBLICAL MODEL
FOR AWAKENING
SOULS

WE HAVE BEGUN TO BUILD FRIENDSHIPS. WE HAVE INITIATED SPIRITUAL CON-
versations. Our friend knows we are a Christian and has felt cared for by
us. Where do we go from here? How do we move forward in the relationship and the conversation? Do we just wait until our friends start asking
questions or move into crisis or enter a new stage of life where they feel
their need for God?

Most of us get stuck at this point. We aren't sure what to do next. There
is a huge untapped potential among Christians who are in relationship with
pre-Christians and who don't know what to do next.

Are you at that point with any of your friends? I am certainly at that
point with most of my pre-Christian friends. What could help us move forward?

John Wesley understood this dilemma. He realized that friendship alone
was not enough. People needed to be awakened to their need for God.
They needed to become anxious for their souls. Today, too, people need to

get more in touch with their spiritual hungers and needs and longings. And then they need to become intrigued with the idea that Jesus might have something to do with meeting their spiritual needs and longings.

In the old model of evangelism, we build friendships, call people to conversion at some evangelistic event and then involve them in Christian fellowship and discipleship. In this model, most of our outreach events are designed for people who are almost ready to fall into the kingdom. They have already come a long way toward Christ. Church services are designed for Christians but can be helpful to people ready to commit themselves to Christ. Programs like Alpha (see appendix four), which extends over a ten-week period and focuses a lot on Jesus and who he was and why he died, are fabulous for people who are already spiritual seekers. But we often lack events that help people initially get interested in and intrigued by God.

We lack what Wesley called "awakening" events, what I am calling *soul-awakening* events and efforts. These events awaken people to the existence of their soul. These events get people in touch with their spiritual needs and longings. These events do *not* call people to conversion. A quick call to conversion is not good servanthood to people who are still a long way from God. It turns them off. It pushes them away.

I am convinced that high-quality soul-awakening events are our greatest missing link in evangelism today.

I am also convinced that high-quality soul-awakening events will be the most controversial part of what vibrant evangelistic ministries do.

Radical Witness
In soul-awakening events we bring the Christian community into the pre-Christian world. We use methods of communication that pre-Christian people respond to. We talk about topics and issues and struggles that face pre-Christian people. Getting into the world of the pre-Christian is the hardest and greatest servanthood we practice in evangelism. And becoming excellent at communicating in ways pre-Christians respond to will cost a lot and challenge us deeply. While we are becoming a community immersed in the world of the pre-Christian in order to reach the pre-Christian, we will also need to remain rooted in Christ and the kingdom of God, with its values that often run counter to the values of the world around us.

Who is adequate for such a challenge? None of us are. But this challenge is nothing less than the Great Commandment, to love God radically and to love our neighbor with abandon.

Paul practiced this kind of radical witness in Acts 17. He got into the pre-Christian world and communicated effectively. He was in Athens, at the Areopagus, and had been traveling around the city. He was feeling blown away and angry at all the idolatry he had seen. Athenians spent all their time telling or hearing about new things, the author of the book of Acts tells us. What a great picture of a postmodern world! Paul was torn and twisted up inside when he saw all the idolatry. But look how he approaches these people and chooses to love and affirm them. Paul puts on a soul-awakening event in the Areopagus, and it works!

I want to look carefully at this event because often people committed to the Bible have a lot of questions about ministries that put on good soul-awakening (or seeker-targeted) events. Paul can help us see the dangers but embrace the good in this approach.

Paul affirms the Athenians' religious orientation. They are seekers. Maybe they are empty-headed seekers, idolatrous, arrogant and misguided. But Paul does not start there. He affirms what he can. He sees their good desire and spiritual hunger.

Paul picks up the signpost in their culture that points to the true God. It is the altar of the unknown god. Rather than excoriating them for their many deities, he zeroes in on the one that has potential to point them to Christ.

He then points them away from their idolatry and toward God and his Son. Here's the gist of his message:

> The Creator who made everything does not live in shrines made by human hands, nor is he served by human hands. For goodness' sake, he gave life to all mortals and all things. How could he need us to give him life if he gave us life?
>
> He gave us life that we might seek him, grope for him, find him. For indeed, as even your poets have said, he is not far from each of us. In him we live and move and have our being (Bible). We are God's offspring (Greek poets).
>
> So we should not think God is like a gold or silver image we make and then worship. That is ignorance. God has overlooked our ignorance in the past, but no longer.
>
> Now God has sent a man to judge the world, and has assured us of this man's role by raising him from the dead.

In response to Paul's words about Jesus' resurrection, some scoff, but others want to hear more.

Paul leaves.

Some people become believers.

Helpful Principles

What principles of soul-awakening events can we draw from Paul's experience?

1. *Paul connects to and affirms the Athenians' culture and uses their language and methods of communication where he can.* He speaks in the Areopagus, as other people do who want to discuss new ideas. He uses rhetorical patterns of communication that are familiar to the Athenians. He uses examples from the Athenians' own context.

2. *Paul discerns and affirms the Athenians' spiritual interest and search.* He chooses to like them and let them know that he likes them. He affirms what he can and builds on common ground. He proposes to answer a question that they have already been asking: who is the unknown god above and beyond all the other gods?

3. *Paul challenges their foolish way of trying to fulfill their search and satisfy the hunger of their souls.* He does so by quoting their own authorities and reasoning in a way that would make sense to his hearers. At first he obeys their rules of truth and doesn't make them first agree to his. They look to their own poets as authority figures, so Paul quotes their poets. They think logically and philosophically, so Paul reasons logically and philosophically. He gets them to admit what they already feel, and then, after confronting their inadequate answers, he begins to share his own ideas.

4. *Paul gives them some surprising evidence that supports his message and points to an unexpected way to fulfill their spiritual search—through Jesus.*

Paul's model is a great one for us as we begin to plan soul-awakening events. He uses the Athenian culture powerfully, but does not thereby lose his essential distinctiveness as a biblical Christian.

In the next chapter we will look at how some current ministries are applying these principles in order to pull off outstanding soul-awakening events. If we can learn from these ministries and develop great soul-awakening events for the people we're trying to reach, a time of great reaping may lie ahead for our church or ministry.

We will use Paul's model as a grid for evaluating these cutting-edge ministries. In so doing we'll avoid some of the dangers we face when we use the instruments and ideas of our culture to reach people.

Discussion Questions

1. Read Acts 17:16-34. How does Paul respond to Athenian culture? What does he do? Where do you agree or disagree with my interpretation of Paul's model?

2. Which aspects of Paul's message surprise you?

3. What idols—things that people wrap their lives and identities around—exist on your campus or in your community? How do you respond?

4. How can we learn from Paul's model of identifying spiritual hunger?

8

AWAKENING SOULS BY CONNECTING TO THE CULTURE

So let's try to imitate Paul. First, how do we connect to and affirm the culture and use the language and methods of communication of the people we're trying to reach?

To answer this question (taking our cue from Paul), we must identify the language people use today to talk about moral and spiritual things. What is the language of moral discourse, of identity formation and of spiritual longing in our culture? We need to consider this if we want to speak to people using words that they will hear, understand and respond to.

Once we identify the language of moral and spiritual discourse in our culture, we will need to use the arts in effective and powerful ways as part of the means of our communication. Chapter three, you'll remember, addresses the importance of capturing the spiritual and moral imagination of people today.

The Language of Therapy

Psychology provides the language of moral discourse and identity formation in our culture. We live in a therapeutic age. Churches and ministries that want to speak to the soul of this generation need to be able to talk about identity and relationships using language from the field of counseling.

Leaders at Willow Creek Community Church, a large evangelistic church in the northwest suburbs of Chicago, have learned to speak this language of emotion and identity and to bring biblical wisdom to these issues. Senior pastor Bill Hybels regularly addresses issues such as personal identity, temperament, family history, the importance of emotions, self-analysis, addiction, self-esteem, boundaries, and control and conflict resolution (Pritchard, pp. 155-56). He is able to use psychological terminology and insight to build a bridge to his audience as he looks at the Scriptures.

The use of our culture's language and awareness of its insights are major reasons Willow Creek's weekend seeker services are outstanding soul-awakening events. Later in the chapter we will consider the dangers in using the language and insights of the culture and see how Paul avoided potential pitfalls. But the challenge of connecting to the culture is still worth discussing.

Hybels gets rid of Christian clichés. Both Christians and pre-Christians find him fun to listen to because he translates Christian ideas using language from the marketplace, the entertainment world, the world of sports. Hybels speaks conversationally, and he liberally sprinkles his messages with humorous, self-deprecating anecdotes. Likewise, Marshall McLuhan has shown that in television we have a "cool medium . . . in which intimate conversation, relaxed discussion, and humor play a more effective role than fiery rhetoric" (quoted in Pritchard, p. 131).

A Language of the Soul

Television and the media have revolutionized the way people learn and change. People learn by identifying with characters in stories. They learn from fellow travelers. They learn in dialogue. The heated rhetoric of the past that filled stadiums and gathered crowds on street corners has been replaced by the intimate, cool communication of the talk show. (For instance, Billy Graham's ministry has become softer, more intimate, more mellow.) The television has transformed even stadium communication. People want to be touched and inspired, not exhorted and preached at. People want an experience more than an explanation, a memorable image more than mere information.

Today's language of spiritual longing is a language about the soul and about having personal power to create our own spiritual reality. The Christian language of lordship, submission, hierarchy, revelation and authority is foreign to the postmodern consciousness. We can't start with that language or assume it means the same thing to the postmodern as it does to us. Obviously we have to get to those ideas, but if people hear that language as they enter the door, the exit sign will be the most noticeable symbol they encounter.

The arts combine image and idea and enhance communication through storytelling and identification. The arts dust off the soul, move us with feelings that transcend us, lower our defenses, draw us in and uncover the longings of our hearts in the daily stuff of our lives.

When students come to another great soul awakening event, InterVarsity Christian Fellowship's "The Edge" at UCLA, the music they first hear is music that they listen to regularly. The emcee is fresh and authentic; the speaker is vulnerable and a little extreme. She shares her struggles and pain and tells humorous anecdotes about herself. She understands that no real communication or influence will happen until she gets over the trust hump. Postmodern people don't tend to trust authority figures. They don't trust people with an agenda. Vulnerability and humor that create a level playing field are key aspects of trust building with people in a postmodern world.

Leaders of the Campus Crusade ministry at UW-Madison have become masters at this kind of vulnerability and humor. Before the speaker came up at Campus Crusade's first meeting of the year, the group was treated to a homemade video of the speaker wearing crazy swimming gear, floating in a pool. He looked like a regular guy who was willing to be embarrassed to build trust. When he came up to speak, the students felt immediately connected to him. There was trust: any older person willing to look foolish couldn't be all bad. "Maybe he is enough like me," says the postmodern student, "that I could learn something from him. And he certainly won't speak down to me, not after he just gave me such an embarrassing picture of himself!"

As people hear their language and encounter forms of communication they are used to, they will trust that we like them and can affirm much in their world. They will feel safe and so will open up to hear a dangerous message. As people hear their language and see the arts used well, the bridge is there for us to begin to look at their spiritual needs and longings.

Finding Common Ground

How do we discern and affirm people's spiritual interest and search? How can we show postmodern people we like them and identify with them? How can we build on common ground? How can we answer questions they already have?

One sad fact is that many people trying to reach the experiential and community-seeking postmodern person don't even seem to like that kind of person. I have good friends in ministry who get so irritated at the way postmodern people think. They believe postmodern people *don't* think. They see postmodern people as lost in an experiential world of emotion and subjectivity, unwilling or unable to think a clear thought if their lives depended on it.

Paul, I think, struggled with indignation over the idolatry and empty-headedness of the Athenians. But he found things to affirm and like, and he started his communication focusing on these things.

I happen to love postmodern experiential and community-seeking people. I love the way they think, feel, imagine and commit. This generation of people understand that a picture can be worth a thousand words. They value authenticity as their highest ethic. They can't stand hypocrisy, cant or "playing politics." They tend to be inclusive, passionate for fairness, committed to reconciliation in relationships. They are highly motivated toward community and are very aware of actions that break trust and community. They honor the beliefs and choices of other people. They tend to want experience before explanation because they want truth that works and reality that rings true.

Those are great qualities. Sure, they need to be balanced by the other side. No matter how much we want to, we cannot completely create our own reality, our own identity, our own spirituality. Words give meaning to images. Sometimes postmodern community encourages enmeshed relationships rather than truly healthy interdependent relationships. Sometimes tolerance embraces the self-destructive in others—not a very loving thing to do.

As G. K. Chesterton said, "The problem with tolerance is not that people will believe nothing, but that they will believe anything."

But the modern mindset had its own strengths and weaknesses. Many of my friends love those modernist rational, analytical strengths and are tolerant of modernist weaknesses like unhealthy individualism, autonomy and a critical spirit. They love to reach people who want evidence and logic and concepts first. But they can get angry and intolerant of postmodern people.

To reach postmodern people, we must see the good, the true, the beautiful, the prophetic that they bring to our lives and our world. We won't reach them until we really like them!

Ministry Starting with Felt Need

We must begin the dialogue at the point of people's interest and need. Here is the felt-need approach to ministry, an approach that Jesus clearly practiced but that the church often rejects and criticizes. Jesus' contemporaries questioned Jesus constantly about his "innovations" in faith that made God more accessible to the unchurched (unsynagogued?) people of his day. Jesus seemed to play it fast and loose on the sabbath. He was much more concerned about inner attitude than about outer ceremony. He dressed like a peasant and invited other peasants to join him in his adventure with God.

The religious people all thought Jesus did a lot of things in the wrong way and at the wrong place and time. He healed at the wrong times. He preached in the wrong ways. He got upset at the wrong things and the wrong people. Why, he had the audacity to throw out all those commercially successful and creative vendors from the temple court just because they made it hard for worthless Gentiles to worship God!

The most controversial things Jesus did had to do with the way he met the felt needs of the poor, the unclean, the lost and the sick. He made the fundamentalists of his day furious.

We too will face the fury of the traditionalists among us if we get serious about meeting the felt needs of the least and the lost.

John Wesley got criticized mostly for what he did in his soul-awakening events. He went to the poor, preaching in fields and open-air spaces. This major innovation reached many unchurched people and was roundly condemned by conservative church leaders and theologians. Wesley believed that if no one was throwing rocks or darts at you, you must be doing something wrong. You must not really be a threat to the status quo, the kingdoms of this world. That doesn't mean that if people are throwing rocks or darts, we are necessarily getting it right! But from the biblical point of view, the absence of controversy is not necessarily a good sign.

Most leaders of ministries that have developed excellent soul-awakening events get a lot of criticism for it. People think they are too superficial. They use too much contemporary language. They uncritically adopt the insights of marketing and the tools of mass communication.

Certainly there are dangers and risks. Greg Pritchard has studied Willow Creek and suggests that seeker-targeted churches can adopt the insights and tools of the culture uncritically, particularly the assumptions of psychology and marketing strategy. Pritchard points out that when we start to use psychological language and ideas to reach people, we can end up taking our ethics from psychology rather than Scripture. We can become more concerned with setting good boundaries and fulfilling ourselves than with taking up our cross and finding our life by losing our life.

We can use the media to create an image that will appeal to non-Christians. But the medium can become the message, and image can lead to pretense and manipulation.

We can use the insights from marketing in uncritical ways. Pre-Christians want to be fulfilled. They want relationships and belonging. They want their felt needs met. We can get so focused on meeting their needs for relationships and fulfillment that we turn relationships into our product and promise self-fulfillment in unbiblical ways. Then we may test our success only by numbers. All of these temptations arise when we adopt a marketing approach to "doing church."

But we have Jesus as our example of proper balance. He profoundly understood his culture. After meeting felt needs of the lost and the least, he brought them to points of crisis. He would feed them with bread and encourage them with the good news of the advent of God's rule and God's justice, but then he would challenge them. He would ask them to think about why they followed him. Was it just because they were fed, just because their felt needs were met?

Jesus didn't adopt the culture in order to ultimately adapt to it and sell out. He had a profound critique of the culture that went hand in hand with a profound ability to adopt the culture and meet felt needs in order to reach people.

If we don't start by meeting people's felt needs, we won't have anybody to talk to. That is where many critics of Willow Creek and the seeker church movement are. They are talking to themselves. They are convincing people to stay behind higher and higher walls of intellectual and moral isolation.

At the same time, if we commit ourselves to meeting people's felt needs and never face the crisis of the cross and self-sacrifice, we will find ourselves trying to make citizens of heaven who will feel equally comfortable in hell. From long involvement with Willow Creek and Saddleback Church, I don't think these churches are doing that. They are emphasizing discipleship, worship, Scripture and ministry to the poor just as much as evangelism. But their heart for the lost genuinely fuels their decisions to serve people and get into their world.

So the question we face as we adapt the culture to reach people is whether in the end people face the cross and the call to sacrifice and are called and helped to become like Jesus. But we need to start with where people are if we want to have any "butts in the seats" (a quote from the movie *Sister Act!*) or any response when we engage them out in the broader world.

Here are the felt needs summarized by Pritchard (pp. 70-73):

1. *Personal fulfillment.* Seventy-two percent of Americans spend much of their time thinking about themselves and their own happiness.

2. *Identity.* Personal identity has become a much more self-created and thus rather tenuous affair.

3. *Companionship.* Gallup concludes that Americans are, in fact, the loneliest people in the world.

4. *Marriage.* Interpersonal intimacy has become the main vehicle for personal fulfillment.

5. *Family.* Even boomer men who are uninterested in church want their children to get religious training.

6. *Relief of stress.* The pace of life and rising expectations for emotional fulfillment have led to highly stressed-out lives.

7. *Meaning and morality.* Lee Strobel puts it this way: Unchurched Harry (the person Willow Creek is trying to reach) is morally adrift, but he secretly wants an anchor.

Postmoderns have one felt need that rises above all the other needs. Postmoderns need belonging and relationship and community. They find fulfillment through relationships, even more than the generation that came before them. As noted in chapter three, people today are looking for a safe place to work out their identity in community.

We need to take this into account in our ethnically diverse world. Many of us are called to reach diverse people. Too many churches settle for reaching only one kind of person. Focus can help us. But in a world where the gospel has often lost its credibility because of Christians' racism and homogeneity, many of us are called to reach out across cultural and ethnic boundaries. We will need the wisdom of those who understand the felt needs and language of diverse ethnic people. Otherwise we will reach only one kind of person and will end up with very homogeneous ministries.

The other great felt need of postmoderns not listed above is the need for spirituality and spiritual insight. Postmodern people are spiritually hungry, open people. They want to create and control their spirituality. They don't want a hierarchical spirituality. But they are hungry. And that spiritual hunger is exciting.

Ministries effectively reaching postmodern people realize that felt needs of pre-Christian people are human needs. They are needs for belonging, relationship, community, identity, spirituality and an experience of the transcendent. If we meet these needs well, we will be meeting the needs of Christians also. Ministries that have learned well how to meet these profound human needs, using Scripture but speaking in the language and mindset of people today, are growing explosively and seeing many people come home to God.

One final comment on Willow Creek and the churches that have modeled themselves after it: the use of the arts, storytelling, practical Christian faith, and authentic sharing of pain and personal experience makes Willow Creek quite effective for postmodern people. The folks at Willow Creek are also reaching modern-mindset people through a logical, rational defense of Christian faith that emphasizes evidence. Their ministry to twenty- to thirty-year-olds (generation X) emphasizes community and small group relationships more than their ministry to people forty to sixty years old (boomers). In that way Willow Creek stands somewhere in between a modern-mindset ministry and a postmodern-mindset ministry. Its style of professionalism, high performance values, excellence and jazz or pop rock music is better for boomers. And so it has launched a ministry to generation X that is stylistically more energetic and raw, and less polished and professional.

Events to Awaken the Soul

So launch some great soul awakening events. Start with a series on relationships. You could call it "How to Be a Great Lover."

Deal with questions of fulfillment, identity, belonging, purpose in life, stress and spirituality. Notice how the culture is dealing with those issues. John Gray's books on Mars and Venus have exploded in sales. He is meeting a felt need. Adapt his ideas. Give him credit. Bring him into your community to sign books at the local bookstore and to speak. Then search the Scriptures for wisdom about how men and women relate to each other. Some sample talks are provided in appendix five.

Use the next *Star Wars* movie, or the past ones, to tap into and talk about our longing for the spiritual. Think about how to acknowledge the interest in ESP and angels and the paranormal and affirm the spiritual interest and hunger it points to, just as Paul did as he looked at the many gods of the Athenians. Yoda can be a great introductory image of Jesus. Truth and power come in very surprising packages. Neo or Morpheus in *The Matrix* can serve as great initial images of Jesus. The truth is what sets us free. We must identify truth, especially spiritual truth, in our quest for freedom.

But don't start by comparing Morpheus and Jesus—direct comparisons are predictable and unhelpful. Identify experiential truths from the life of Morpheus first; then bring Jesus in not as a cliché comparison but as a surprising, stereotype-breaking experience. We might say, "Morpheus is the mentor who helps Neo face hard realities. We all need mentors like that, don't we? Let me share about a mentor who unexpectedly helped me face my hard realities." Then we could share a difficult experience from our past that Jesus guided us through.

Use Laurie Beth Jones's material on defining personal mission. Do an evening seminar on finding a personal mission. But make sure to glean wisdom from Scripture. Give examples of the life mission of people you know and then of biblical characters. David's life mission was to be a man of integrity, after God's own heart. For Paul, "to live is Christ, to die is gain." If you share these as stories, without initially preaching at people, people will be challenged just by the examples.

Debates can also be great soul-awakening events. Invite an apologist like William Lane Craig to debate a notorious local atheist, or Haman Cross Jr. to debate a local Muslim leader.

You could sponsor a series for families on meeting the spiritual and moral needs of their children. Invite all the people who have just started having kids in your neighborhood and community. Even if they haven't pursued their own spiritual needs, they often care about their kids' spiritual needs, and many pre-Christians return to church at that point in their lives. One church drew over five hundred people for a seminar on potty training, because that was the greatest felt need the parents in their community had! A group of African American and Latino students that I know developed a soul-awakening event about our need for a good father. It was powerful!

Especially look to meet the needs of people in transition. That is when they become receptive to life change. When they've moved or experienced loss or entered college or just had kids or retired, they are profoundly open to things that will help meet their new needs and their longing for deeper meaning. Any church or ministry that meets needs of people in transition has fabulous potential for growth and for seeing many people come home to God.

You can host meetings on reconciling relationships. Include help for estranged friendships, strained family-of-origin relationships, struggling marriages and tense interracial relationships. Offer help for people experiencing relational loss or breakup.

You can use culturally accepted means that are also spiritually powerful. Partner with a local gospel choir to reach your campus or community. Make sure the gospel choir members share their story of Jesus' vibrant work in their lives. Many pre-Christian people today will come to a gospel choir concert. It's a cultural "thing" that God can use to reach postmodern people.

Get a psychologist from your church to work with you on a biblical perspective on identity formation. A college Christian group recently offered a meeting on "Unwrapping Your True Self." They drew scores of college students through the publicity alone—which is highly unusual. Generally people come to events because friends invite them. Never count on publicity alone to build your attendance. But when people come out in response to your publicity, you've hit on a very intense felt need.

Sponsor a movie discussion before or between your Sunday services. You might be surprised at how many people are interested! Encourage people to take their friends to the movie the night before.

Offer seminars and practical help for troubled teens, or single moms, or relationships rocked by racial tension. One church in Dallas, Texas, designates male deacons to help, love and discipline teen boys with no male presence at home. That church has seen many single moms flock to services, seek help and pursue Jesus in new ways.

You can also take a walk through Borders or Barnes & Noble or multiplex movie theaters, looking for what is striking a chord and thinking about how you could use it to reach your postmodern friends. Think about the truths in popular books and film. Every culture contains experiential truth that is true to Christian faith and the gospel. God has put his image in humans, and his handprints are all over our cultures.

The possibilities for great soul awakening events are endless. Go for it!

Discussion Questions

1. Evaluate your most public services or meetings. How do pre-Christians feel when they attend? Are visitors welcome?

2. Do your services rely on insider language and Christian clichés?

3. What do you think are the most important felt needs of the pre-Christian people around you? How do they talk about those needs, and how do they talk about spiritual things? You can refer back to pages 81-83.

4. Who are the people in transition in your community? What are their felt needs and how could you meet them? How could you draw those people toward Jesus?

5. What are the books people are reading, the movies they are watching, the music they are listening to? What do these things tell you about their needs, interests and spiritual concerns?

6. Choose a movie. What truths about life and relationships are expressed in this movie? How could you develop a soul-awakening event using it? What can you affirm in the movie? Where could the movie help you challenge people on the foolish ways they are seeking to fulfill their spiritual and emotional needs? How could you begin to talk about Jesus in relation to the themes of the movie? Appendix five presents a process for building a soul-awakening event around a felt need. A sample outline is also included.

7. What soul-awakening events could you or your ministry work on that would reach the people you are trying to reach? Who might work with you on a team to develop some great events? What are your next steps?

9

AWAKENING SOULS BY CHALLENGING PRE-CHRISTIAN PEOPLE

LET'S CONTINUE LOOKING AT HOW WE CAN IMITATE PAUL IN ACTS 17. WE'VE looked at *connecting to* pre-Christian people today. But we must move on to the stage of *challenging* pre-Christian people.

Posing a Challenge

How do we challenge today's experiential, community-seeking people about their foolish ways of trying to fulfill their search and satisfy the hunger of their souls? How can we confront them using their rules of truth and quoting their authorities? How do we get them to face what they already feel and to admit the inadequacy of their answers, thus becoming open to other ideas?

We must challenge people today. We must ask them stimulating, intriguing, even disturbing questions. Our question to their soul must be: Does this life we're living make any sense? Paul asked this question of the Athenians with great impact.

Does it make any sense to bring our kids up in a world that is sailing into the future without anchor or rudder? With no reference point outside of ourselves, we are drifting into the shoals of teen violence, sexual disease, environmental disaster, political amorality.

We face a crisis of character at every level of society. Can we survive the crisis? Does it make any sense to foster the kind of tolerance that is rootless and will lead us to wither and fade as a culture?

Does it make any sense that we have come of age in usurping control over the process of evolution through gene mapping and technology, even as we regress toward infancy in our moral and ethical capacity?

Does it make any sense that we believe in the unrestricted expression of our sexual needs and the unhindered effort at our self-fulfillment, resulting in relational disasters that leave us hurting and unfulfilled?

Does it make any sense that as we claim the capacity to name ourselves and determine our own identity, we are becoming more confused than ever about who we are?

Does It Make Any Sense?

As we challenge the postmodern mindset, we need first to use postmodern rules of truth, just like Paul first used the rules of truth and quoted the authorities of the Athenians as much as he could. We need to ask whether what we're saying rings true to the experiential, community-seeking person. Does it make emotional and experiential sense? Remember, people today are on a search for what rings true to their lives.

When we begin by arguing from our truth basis—the Bible, revelation, modernist kinds of evidence—we lose the people we are trying to reach. We need to argue *to* our truth basis, as Paul did, not *from* our truth basis.

Rules of Experiential Truthtelling

That's one reason storytelling is important. Storytelling helps us follow the rules of experiential truth. If something rings true for us experientially and we can be authentic and nonmanipulative in the way we tell the story, people will respond.

Movies can serve as training wheels in teaching us to follow the rules of experiential truth. A good movie communicates a compelling vision of truth. It does so by telling a story that rings true and that echoes in our experience and in our souls. Today, movies that don't communicate relational, emotional and psychological truth often don't succeed well. The first installment of the second Star Wars trilogy was weak on character, on story, on emotional and psychological truth. Though the movie was financially successful and visually stimulating, it was relationally boring and therefore a disappointment for many.

What is *experientially and emotionally* true or real, what rings true, is immensely important to people today. The understanding of truth has changed, and so we must change the way we communicate truth. As Ravi Zacharias asks us, "How do we communicate truth to a generation that hears with their eyes and thinks with their feelings?"

We can take people a long way toward the confessional truths of Christian faith using experiential truth. That's what great soul-awakening events do. But how do we learn to think in the language and by the rules of experiential truth? And then how do we argue *to* our truth basis, the Scriptures? I helped to draft this list of "experiential truth rules" with a group of Inter-Varsity staff hosted by Doug Schaupp and Jenny Vaughan at UCLA.

1. *Don't invalidate the experience of others.* We want to challenge them in ways that help them reframe their experiences. But at this stage we are not trying to invalidate their experiences.

2. *Bank on the fact that people have a soul and spiritual interest and hunger.* If they are willing to come to your event, that says a lot! What's more, they are human, and humans have souls and spiritual longings. Count on it, and affirm every evidence you see in them.

3. *Appeal to commonly shared authorities, to postmodern prophets* in music and the movies. Turn to shared universal truth experiences, events in our culture, movies that have become part of our story as a culture. The key hump to get over is to recognize that God's image is reflected in this culture and that there are many cultural elements or "handles" we can use to awaken spiritual interest and connect that interest to God.

4. *Help people get in touch with their longing, their yearning, their emptiness.* Often you can do this by telling your story, or through good drama, or by pointing out the longings expressed by the characters in a compelling movie.

5. *Win your emotional and experiential truth points first,* before you bring in Jesus and the Bible. Here is where you are arguing *to* your truth basis, not *from* it. Convince people of their need for a leader, a mentor, a guide or a forgiver from your own life or from the movie or drama you are using,

before you start talking about Jesus.

6. *Tie Jesus and the Bible not to propositional truths but to experiential truth moments from your own life and from shared stories,* such as movies or personal experiences. Don't bring in the propositions based on some outside authority. People will experience that as a bait and switch. When I want to start talking about Jesus in a message, I either use a short drama or start with a struggle I faced and tell how Jesus helped in a *very* unexpected way. People are just waiting for you to bring in Jesus in a cliché way. So I often tell how my encounter *with* Jesus blew away all my stereotypes *of* Jesus.

7. *Create a transformational moment and then interpret it.* The transformational moment is that point in the event when people sense that God might be present and are given space to deal with God themselves. Bring people to that point with a good drama, a powerful song, or a haunting, soul-searching question. You have shared your story, been honest about your pain. Now you have earned the right to get into their lives. "Your soul is opening up right now. You've related to some of this. God is tapping you on your shoulder. Will you turn and deal?" Questions are often at the heart of these transformational moments. Asking a powerful, poignant question can help bring the work of the Spirit in the life of the pre-Christian to a very intense and transforming moment.

8. *Work deeply with the transformational moment.* Share what you are going through at the transformational moment. Express how deeply the question you have just asked moves you and challenges your own soul. Then turn it into a challenge to your hearers' souls. "I want to be loved when I am unlovable. Can your soul handle more love? Or will you shut down, stay lonely, wall yourself off from God and from others?"

9. *If you practice smooth transitions, you can be very challenging and prophetic at the transformational moment.* What I mean by *transitions* is key points at which you shift the focus toward your main point and toward Jesus. Let's say you started the event with a drama about relational struggles, and then you told a story of a relational breakup in your life. How you begin to talk about the healing process and about Jesus is very important. Smooth transitions don't interrupt the flow of experiential truth. People stay with you because what you are sharing continues to ring true experientially, emotionally, psychologically and spiritually.

For example: "I read the Bible sometimes to get wisdom for life. Just when I was devastated over this breakup, I found a woman in the Bible who had experienced the same kind of relational chaos I had. Can you believe it? The Bible very unexpectedly spoke to my pain and chaos by giving me an example of someone who was just as messed up as I was. That woman appears in our next drama." A drama based on Jesus' encounter with the Samaritan woman in John 4 can follow—but make sure it incorporates some unexpected contemporary dialogue. Now Jesus has been introduced into the discussion in a way that honors the rules of experiential truth.

After the soul-awakening event, provide avenues of follow-up through community for pre-Christians who attended. Offer to have coffee and conversation with them. Open up GIGs (groups investigating God) or an Alpha course as the next step. When you follow the rules of experiential truth, you will build the trust needed to draw people into community. Don't squander that opportunity! The next chapter will give you lots of help with this step.

I have come to believe we waste a lot of time, energy and resources if we don't have a well-developed follow-up strategy to soul awakening. An ongoing experience of community designed with the questions of seekers in mind will serve the needs of earnest pre-Christians.

If you have no way to draw people into seeking community, don't bother with these events. They will be a lot of work and won't bear fruit.

Presenting Evidence

How do we offer surprising evidence that supports our ideas and that points to an unexpected way to fulfill people's spiritual search, through Jesus? What kinds of evidence are experiential, community seeking postmodern people looking for?

Alister McGrath suggests that postmodern people's first question is not "Is it true?" in the conceptual or philosophical sense. They have two prior questions.

1. *Is it attractive?* Does it bring relational harmony? Does it enrich human life? Would it enrich my life?

2. *Is it relevant?* Does it work? Would it make my life better? Would it improve society?

After these questions are addressed, they will be open to asking, "Is it true?" in a more conceptual or evidential sense.

Attractiveness, relevance, harmony and utility are truth questions for postmoderns, so there is no actual dichotomy between those questions and the truth question. The evidence postmoderns will respond to is evidence of the attractiveness and relevance, harmony and utility of a conviction. Once this evidence is demonstrated, more logical proof will be compelling. But until the evidence for the attractiveness and relevance of Christian faith has been presented, logical proofs will make little impact.

Thus when we face questions about sexuality or racism or sexism or spirituality, or when we are pointing people to Jesus, we need to address attractiveness and relevance issues first.

Homosexually oriented people will look at our lives before they listen to our words. Have we ministered to those with AIDS? How can we share our own sexual struggles? How can we first treat homosexually oriented people as people who have been met with unjust and horrifying hatred and revulsion? That approach isn't guaranteed to win trust, nor does it address every issue. The homosexual agenda would remake our society and confirm autonomous human ability to determine human identity without regard to God, which we can't affirm. But how can we lead with love?

Some Christians are called to fight the political battle before they fight the evangelistic battle of offering love and acceptance. And homosexually oriented folk will feel rage at those people. That's a cost for that more political prophetic calling. But some, like the apostle Paul, are called to make it their priority to proclaim the good news to gays. And we must first *be* good news before we can tell good news. We must answer the attractiveness and relevance questions before we take on the truth and limits questions. Those who are called to a prophetic stand are first called to demonstrate radical love and servanthood. Otherwise their prophetic stance will merely be heard as hatred.

The same can be said with regard to racial issues. Racial reconciliation is a biblical priority for discipleship, but it is also an urgent priority for evangelism. Our past racism has undermined our credibility and obscured the gospel.

Some years ago I helped lead a great soul awakening event, a prayer gathering in downtown Chicago. The prayer leaders were African American, Asian American, Hispanic American, Anglo and international. We were Baptist, Presbyterian, Pentecostal, Methodist, Episcopalian, Catholic and nondenominational. God was delighted, and people, including pre-Christian people, were deeply moved and inspired toward relationship with God. We repented of racial and religious prejudice. We worshiped together, led by a gospel choir. We expressed our concern for the poor by bringing canned goods to donate. We were attractive, relevant and true to our world. That's evangelism postmodern people are drawn to like a magnet!

In your events, tell how you expected Jesus to be unattractive and irrelevant, and how you were surprised by his reality, his attractive and winsome personality, his capacity to enjoy life, his unbelievable response to hurting and messed-up folk. Then present your evidence and your logic to opened-up hearts.

Attractiveness and relevance first. That's the evidence our postmodern friends will hear and respond to!

A Summary of Paul's Model

First, Paul connected to and affirmed the Athenians' culture, using their own language and methods of communication where he could.

Second, Paul discerned and affirmed their spiritual interest and search.

Third, Paul confronted their foolish way of trying to fulfill their search and satisfy the hunger of their souls. But he did so using their rules of truth and quoting their authorities as much as possible.

Finally, Paul offered some surprising evidence that supported his message and pointed to an unexpected way to fulfill the Athenians' spiritual search, through Jesus.

Go for it! Imitate Paul in using the culture and its forms to reach people. Imitate Jesus in meeting felt needs and then challenging people to follow the way of the cross.

Hold great soul-awakening events monthly, or as often as you can with excellence. Invite people into community as a next step. Work together with a team. And God *will* bless you. Soul-awakening events are an exciting cutting edge of evangelism in the twenty-first century.

Discussion Questions

1. How do you respond to the rules of experiential truthtelling mentioned on pages 93-96?

2. In light of Alister McGrath's suggested "attractiveness, relevance, then logic and evidence" communication model, how might you reach out to people across racial boundaries or to homosexual strugglers?

10

DEVELOPING GENUINE CHRISTIAN COMMUNITY

IF SOUL-AWAKENING EVENTS ARE THE LEADING EDGE AND MISSING LINK IN evangelism, drawing people into seeking community is the heart and soul of evangelism today. If you implement only one of the steps of this book, I encourage you to implement this one! And I encourage you never to sponsor an event or hold an outreach meeting without having in place a way to draw pre-Christians into seeking community.

Groups investigating God (GIGs) and the Alpha course, explained later, are two powerful and effective ways of drawing pre-Christians into seeking community. The next chapter and the appendixes will give you some stories and lots of help for these efforts. But first let's focus some energy and attention on the *priority and quality* of the community we want to draw pre-Christian people into.

The Priority of Community

Today people are looking for a community to belong to before a message to believe in. Evangelism is about helping people belong so that they come to believe. Most people today do not "decide" to believe. In community they "discover" that they believe, and then they decide to affirm that publicly and to follow Christ intentionally. People are looking for a safe, accepting place to develop their identity and sense of self in community.

Our friend has now been awakened to his spiritual need. He has begun to connect the satisfaction of that hunger with the possibility of Jesus. But he still has a long way to go. He still carries some negative stereotypes of Christian faith. And he still carries many barriers, trust barriers, that keep him from wholehearted commitment in any direction.

He may have experienced the breakdown of his parents' marriage. He has seen failure and hypocrisy in his leaders—certainly political leaders but also religious leaders. And he is not looking for absolute truth or for someone else to tell him what to do and how to believe. If he wants to be spiritual, he wants to be spiritual on his own terms. Words like *obedience, lordship* and *judgment* still freak him out.

So how do we help our friend go the next steps in the journey toward faith, trust and commitment? Our friend needs to be able to discover truth for himself, in a context where he can talk through his questions and thoughts and experience acceptance and affirmation. Our friend needs to experience our love, but he also needs to experience God's love and reality for himself. He needs to experience the relevance and power of biblical truth and of Jesus for his own life.

In other words, our friend needs to seek and experience spiritual truth and reality in the context of community.

But here we face a major obstacle in our outreach. Our groups and churches often do not offer community that pre-Christian people are attracted to. What keeps us from having the kind of Christian community that pre-Christian people can become part of?

For one, most churches have never learned that, in William Temple's words, "the Church is the only society in the world that exists for its nonmembers" (quoted by Hunter, p. 28). And as John Stott has asked us in a talk I heard years ago, "Are we more like a church, or are we more like a club? A club spends its dues on the needs of the members. A church spends its dues on the needs of the nonmembers." Most churches exist for their members, who feel they never get enough attention. And as Bill Hybels asserted in a recent talk, "The toughest part about building a church that is welcoming to seekers is getting the members to be the workers and funders for a ministry designed with somebody else in mind."

Second, most churches think they already have good fellowship for pre-Christians, if they could only get them there. Few of us are aware of how our group feels to pre-Christian people. But often our language, our acronyms, our announcements, our music, our messages, the way we pray, and our tendency to greet only those we know when we are together put up very noticeable barriers to those who are not yet Christian.

To combat this tendency, one church has a three-minute rule. In the first three minutes after the service is done, members cannot talk to people they already know. They are challenged to meet and welcome the new people. After three minutes most new people have already "escaped," so members can then talk to one another! But this kind of approach is all too rare in our churches and communities.

Jesus shows us the kind of open-hearted community he wants in the small group he led. Certainly he had times alone with the disciples and teaching meant for their ears only. But generally Jesus modeled a radical, highly committed yet highly accessible community life with his disciples.

Jesus came to seek the lost, to heal the sick, to save the sinner. His community was oriented to that priority. He practiced no false dichotomy between evangelism and discipleship. What was discipleship without healing the sick and seeking the lost? It was certainly not what Jesus had in mind. What was community without concrete compassion for the lost? Jesus constantly attacked compassionless community. It was exclusive community that so angered Jesus when he cleansed the temple and cursed the fig tree. God's temple was to be a house of prayer for all the nations. When outsiders could no longer get inside and find God through Israel's worship, it was time for the temple to die. When outsiders can no longer get into our churches and groups and find God, is it time for our church or group to die? How can people be followers of Jesus and yet build exclusive communities so foreign to his character?

Whenever I visit a church, I read their mission statement, and then I look at their programs and ministry to see if there is a match. What I saw today when I visited a church is not unusual. Two-thirds of the mission statement focused on reaching the lost and helping them come to Christ and grow. But when I read about their programs and ministries, apparently about 5 percent was directed at reaching the lost. For many churches, that's high.

So what kind of community will draw postmodern people and help them find God? Seven freshmen at the University of Wisconsin-Madison first modeled for me this kind of winsome community.

I had just started my time there on InterVarsity staff, fresh from my experience as an engineer at Exxon Research and Engineering. As I began my ministry, I was depressed at the quality of the group I was to work with. Large community gatherings were boring and confused. Christians were insecure and weak in commitment, having seen some of their close friends drop out of the faith. Small groups were shrinking. Students were heady but not heartfelt in their approach to their faith. And the group was cliquish. Some pre-Christian students who visited promised me that they would never be back. I prayed my heart out. I didn't know what else to do.

Thankfully, a small group of seven freshman decided to stick it out. They recognized the sorry state of the fellowship as a whole, but they decided to pray instead of leave. They began to hold daily prayer meetings, committing themselves to attend every Tuesday afternoon at 5:30 p.m.

Their prayer times were very simple and heartfelt. They spent ten minutes in simple worship. They spent ten more minutes in honest confession of their sins and weaknesses to God and to one another. And then they spent ten minutes praying for the campus and for their friends. They wanted God to help some of their friends come to know Jesus in a personal love relationship. To make their worship times sweet, they encouraged one of their number, Charlie, to bring his guitar each week.

God began to work in their hearts and convict them. God wanted them to take a risk to reach out to their friends. But what could they do? What event could they invite their friends to in this largely dying fellowship group? Should they ask their friends to come to a large group meeting? These freshmen didn't like the large group meetings. They were part of the fellowship in *spite of* those meetings. They were not proud of them. They would feel embarrassed to bring their friends. The "cringe factor" (how many times Christians cringe during a meeting to which they have brought their friends) was just too high.

Small groups were awkward. Social events were cliquish. These freshmen felt stuck.

Then one of them, Peter, spoke up. "I'm going to bring my friend Dick to this prayer meeting. It's the only thing our fellowship does that seems attractive to me."

Another freshmen objected. "This is a prayer meeting. Your friend is going to feel weird. We're going to feel weird." But Peter was adamant.

True to his word, Peter brought Dick the next Tuesday. At first the freshmen were awkward. But soon they relaxed and prayed as they always had. They worshiped simply. They confessed sin honestly and in simple, specific words. They prayed for their campus and their friends. Peter even prayed for his friend Dick to be encouraged.

We ended the prayer time, and Dick practically tackled Peter and me as we were leaving. "What was that?!" he wanted to know.

We weren't sure what he was asking about. Dick was a cosmic-consciousness, pot-smoking, drug-and-alcohol-using student who had sampled Marxist and New Age thinking and decided to embrace atheism. We wondered if he had slipped out and smoked a joint while we weren't looking.

"What was what?" we asked, somewhat anxiously.

Dick's response: "I don't even believe in God, but God was in that room. What happened?"

Peter and I went on to talk about God's presence and Jesus. We shared the gospel with Dick and invited him to respond. He did. Dick came to know Jesus that night. He went from being an atheist to being a Christian in a three-hour period. That's not supposed to happen!

What convinced him? A group of struggling, authentic, accepting freshmen who had learned how to be people of the Presence. Dick encountered the presence of God in an authentic, Spirit-filled community.

Those freshmen were now jazzed! Every one of them wanted to bring their friends to the prayer meeting. And they did. That year, primarily through that prayer meeting, over twenty-five students came into a love relationship with Jesus. Many of those students today are in urban ministry, missions and leadership in seeker-oriented churches. That year we all became convinced that the most powerful thing we could do was to be honest and authentic in our struggles and seek God's face until he showed up in tangible ways.

That freshman community was marked by

1. humor and humility
2. warmth and acceptance extended to new people
3. authenticity about their lives and their struggles
4. changed lives and genuine Christian experience

5. a tangible sense of God's presence

They were strugglers who could laugh at themselves and affirm other strugglers and who were marked in tangible and transforming ways by the presence of God. They were people of the Presence, with the changed lives to prove it.

What else distinguishes us from all the people of the earth, besides God's presence transforming struggling people?

Moses underlines the importance of God's presence for us as we move forward in mission. After the Israelites sin by fashioning and worshiping the golden calf, God tells Moses, "I will send an angel before you. . . . I will not go up among you, or I would consume you on the way, for you are a stiff-necked people" (Ex 33:3).

Moses asks God to show Moses God's ways, so that Moses can keep God's favor. God then promises to go with Moses. Moses jumps on that one. "If your presence will not go, do not carry us up from here. For how shall it be known that I have found favor in your sight, I and your people, unless you go with me? In this way, we shall be distinct, I and your people, from every people on the face of the earth" (Ex 33:14-16). To paraphrase, "What else will distinguish us from every other people on earth? Your presence, and your presence alone, with us struggling and sinful people!"

In a postmodern world, authentic, Spirit-filled community is the most powerful apologetic we have.

Developing Authentic, Spirit-Filled Community

So how do we grow in becoming strugglers who accept other strugglers and who are marked by this tangible, transforming presence of God?

Paul models well this paradox we are seeking to live. In 2 Corinthians 12:7-10 he explores this fundamental paradox of strength out of weakness.

> To keep me from becoming conceited because of the surpassingly great revelations, there was given me a thorn in the flesh, a messenger of Satan, to torment me. Three times I pleaded with the Lord to take it away from me. But he said to me, "My grace is sufficient for you, for my power is made perfect in your weakness." Therefore I will boast all the more gladly about my weaknesses, so that Christ's power may rest on me. That is why, for Christ's sake, I delight in weaknesses, in insults, in persecutions, in difficulties. For when I am weak, then I am strong.

We are not to glorify weakness and vulnerability as some ministries do these days. We are to glorify God. But we do that best when we boast of our weaknesses and struggles so that God's power and presence will be seen in our weakness.

We can cultivate this kind of winsome weakness in two ways:

1. We need a fresh encounter with Jesus and the Scriptures.
2. We need a fresh taste of genuine Christian experience.

A Fresh Encounter with Jesus and the Scriptures

Many of us grew up thinking we had to have our act together, especially if we grew up in the church. We felt shame whenever we blew it or didn't say it right. We can have a very distorted picture of Jesus: he is always watching, noticing every misstep, failure, sin and performance blunder. We think Jesus is like a stern parent, highly responsible, highly accusatory whenever we err. As a result, we don't want to be around Jesus when we feel weak or vulnerable any more than we want to show that side of who we are to authority figures or friends. When we feel sinful, when we feel like failures, Jesus is the last person we want to be around.

The Gospels give us a very different picture of Jesus and who wanted to be around him. The ashamed woman caught in adultery finds love, forgiveness and hope for better choices in the future. The blind man, whom the disciples try to get rid of and whom the people think is a terrible sinner, finds Jesus asking, "What do you want?" He finds acceptance, healing, hope. Levi/Matthew, whom every true Jew hated because he worked hand in glove with the Roman oppressors, invites Jesus to his home for a delightful supper. Through simple and heartfelt acceptance, Jesus revolutionizes the lives of people locked in shame. Jesus proclaims, "It is not the healthy who need a doctor, but the sick. I have not come to call the righteous, but sinners" (Mk 2:17).

It was the people who had their act together who didn't want to be around Jesus. If you had failed or sinned or felt wounded or inadequate, Jesus was just the kind of person you wanted to be around. He accepted you. He didn't shame you. But if you were arrogant, the type of religious person who made others feel ashamed, worthless, excluded, look out! Jesus had no patience with you. To him you were a whitewashed tomb, a dead branch, a hypocrite playing a part. How we have turned it around in the church! The people who came running to Jesus run away from our fellowships. And the people Jesus sent packing now often pack our pews and chairs.

Are you letting a sin or sense of shame keep you from looking Jesus in the eye? Well look up! Those loving, accepting eyes are filled with compassion for you. And you will take a step closer to the winsome weakness so attractive to pre-Christian people when they see freedom from shame in your eyes.

A Fresh Taste of Genuine Christian Experience

Encountering the real Jesus, the Jesus who loves the ashamed and loathes arrogance, is the first step on the path to experiencing the strength through weakness that will be so winsome to people outside God's family. But after we have looked into the Scriptures, into the eyes of Jesus, how do we go on to encounter this very real, very intriguing and delightful person in ways that become attractive to pre-Christian people?

Here are six significant ways to enter, and invite pre-Christian people to enter, genuine, transforming Christian community and experience.

1. Heartfelt worship. Worship evangelism may be the most significant means of evangelism in the next century, because it combines authenticity and vulnerability with a genuine experience of God's presence. Pre-Christians see who we are and that we genuinely love God. Our relationship to God becomes more real and heartfelt. But we need to worship in ways that are accessible to pre-Christians. That is addressed in the practical section below.

2. Confession of sin—especially to one another. James writes:

> Is any one of you sick? He should call the elders of the church to pray over him and anoint him with oil in the name of the Lord. And the prayer offered in faith will make the sick person well; the Lord will raise him up. If he has sinned, he will be forgiven. Therefore confess your sins to each other and pray for each other, that you may be healed. The prayer of a righteous man is powerful and effective. (Jas 5:14-16)

Those freshmen at Madison knew how to confess sin in a way that was very powerful for themselves and for pre-Christians who came. They kept it simple. They kept it specific. They kept it heartfelt. They didn't use religious language to confess sin. Typically they prayed, "God, forgive me for hurting my roommate," or "God, forgive me for blowing off my studies," or "God, forgive me for my struggle with sex and pornography. God, I need you so much!" Their simple, heartfelt confessions were so powerful for other Christians and for pre-Christians.

As a junior in college, I struggled with sexual temptation. I needed help. When I finally admitted to myself and others that I needed help, I was blown away. Christian friends encouraged me, and pre-Christian friends identified with me.

3. Listening prayer. When we are troubled and we hear God speak directly to our struggle, we are encouraged—and we can share the experience with others.

Recently I led a national conference on evangelism. The morning the conference was to begin, I woke up sick as a dog. I could hardly get out of bed. For a panicky moment, I realized that I might have to miss the conference. The conference would probably have done fine. But I would lose my national debut! "How could you do this to me, God?" I cried out.

Then I listened. On the wall of my hotel room there was a picture of lilies in a field. Suddenly, in a still, small but very penetrating voice, Jesus spoke into my heart: "Consider the lilies. They toil not, neither do they spin. Yet Solomon in all his splendor was not arrayed as one of these."

I was valuable to God. I was valuable whether I was leading a national consultation or laid out sick in a bed. The comfort Jesus gave by speaking that word into my heart was deeply healing and gave me the perspective I needed. God's word to my struggle renewed genuine Christian experience in my life at that moment.

And later I was able to share the experience with a pre-Christian friend. He too was struggling with the value of his life and work. The authentic power of my encounter with God in a struggle we both shared intrigued him greatly.

4. Healing prayer. When God ministers to us where we've been hurt, we can minister to others, Christian and pre-Christian. Healing prayer helps us get excited about how God is working in our own life.

I sat next to a Jewish woman on the plane trip home from a recent conference. She and I began to talk. I spoke about the healing I had experienced during the conference in my attitude toward my dad. She began to tell me about her struggles, especially in her relationship with her dad. Time stood still as we shared and as I talked about God's power to heal. She left deeply moved, committing herself to read the New Testament and look at the life of Jesus for the first time ever. When we experience healing, we have a story to tell that is powerful and attractive to experiential, community-seeking people!

Direct healing prayer for pre-Christians can also be quite powerful. Several years ago I spoke in a dorm at a secular campus on "Does God Heal Today?" Thirty-five students crammed into the dorm lounge. I spoke simply, sharing from the life of Jesus and my own life, and then invited students to receive prayer. I spent until 1:00 a.m. praying for Christians and pre-Christians. It was amazing to see the hunger people had, and to look into their eyes after they felt loved in our prayer time together!

The high point of the Alpha course, dealt with at more length below, is the discussion and experience of the Holy Spirit during the weekend retreat midway through the course. Many people come into the kingdom at that time.

5. *Risk-taking in crossing relational and cultural barriers.* Often when we choose to cross denominational or cultural barriers, our horizons are expanded and our capacity to experience God is enriched. For me, attending a black church with a fabulous gospel choir opened my eyes to new dimensions of worship. Later in my life I joined a sacramental, Spirit-enthused church, and once again my heart was swept up into new realities of worship and experience of God. These experiences gave me new eyes and awareness as I read Scripture. Although I read the same Bible, God spoke to me in profoundly new ways through its pages.

Empathy and appreciation of those different from ourselves can help us immensely in reaching the lost. It also opens our hearts to God in new ways that bubble over into our witness. And many of our pre-Christian friends would love to take this risk with us. They would love to go to a great black church with a fabulous gospel choir. It might be their first experience in church in years, but if visiting this church is new for both of you, they won't feel so self-conscious and afraid of embarrassing themselves.

Remember, people are looking for a safe, accepting community in which to work out their identity. As you experience diversity, and as your community expresses diversity, you become a safe, accepting place for people of other ethnicities, cultures and experiences to come home to God.

6. *Risk-taking in team evangelism out of weakness instead of strength.* Nothing adds dynamism to my Christian walk and testimony like sharing my faith with pre-Christian people. Nothing else makes me feel quite so inadequate and dependent on God.

You might think, *How can you involve pre-Christians in team evangelism, except as the object of your efforts?* When I was coming home to God as a sophomore in college, my friend Jim invited me to join his small group. His small group had a mission. They ran an outreach booktable once a week in the student union. They were an evangelism team. So once a week, as a pre-Christian, I sat at that booktable, giving some good booklets to interested people and hearing Jim and others give some good answers to hard questions. I was part of an evangelism team before I was a Christian!

I don't think anything helps faith grow, Christ come alive, or pre-Christians be struck by our convictions more than this kind of risk-taking team evangelism.

Cautions

Some cautions are needed here. There are some unbalanced ways to seek to encounter Jesus and gain a fresh taste of genuine Christian experience.

We can be power-centered in our approach to God's presence. We can ask God to show up and show off, believing that we want him to show up to impress pre-Christians when actually we want God to show up so we can look good. We may want people to be impressed with God, but it wouldn't hurt if they were also impressed with us, now would it? That dual desire seems to be self-defeating as well as sinful. Paul looked unimpressive so God could look impressive. When people were too impressed with Paul, and especially when Paul started to be too impressed with himself, God sent Paul a thorn in the flesh. The only alternative would have been to stop showing up through Paul. The thorn was probably God's grace to Paul, to keep him in ministry and out of the tabloids of his day!

We can also be experience-centered in our desire for God to show up. We want the experience as an end in itself. God seems to cease responding to such self-centeredness over the long haul. The experience as an end in itself dries up after a few years, months, days or sometimes even moments.

These twin temptations—toward power and toward experience as an end in itself—are, I believe, why many healing movements eventually see God's healing power dry up and then have to manufacture pseudo-healing experiences in order to keep going. That path leads to destruction (or at least to the pages of the *National Enquirer*), and certainly not to life for Christians or for pre-Christians.

Conclusion
Winsome Christian community and tangible encounters with God's presence are at the core of reaching postmodern people today. As we encounter Jesus afresh in the Scriptures, and as we respond together in heartfelt worship, confession of sin, listening prayer, healing prayer, risk-taking in crossing relational barriers and in team evangelism, our Christian experience will become vibrant and contagious. We will have a story to tell and the passion to tell it. We will have vibrant experiences into which to invite our pre-Christian friends.

Discussion Questions
1. Look at 2 Corinthians 12:7-10. Does this experience of strength in the midst of honest sharing of struggles characterize your fellowship or church? Why or why not? How could you grow in this?

2. If you were to face Jesus today, what would he say to you? Is your picture of Jesus consistent with the Gospels' picture of one who transforms those locked in shame and opposes those who assume they have their religious act together?

3. What keys to genuine Christian experience have you experienced? Which ones would you like to grow in? Why? How could you or your group grow in these keys? How could you invite pre-Christians into these events and experiences?

4. Are you a community to which ethnically diverse people would want to come to develop their identity and sense of self and explore their questions about God? Why or why not? How might you want to grow in this regard?

11

DRAWING PRE-CHRISTIANS INTO SEEKING COMMUNITY

SO LET'S GET PRACTICAL. HOW DO WE DRAW PRE-CHRISTIANS INTO HEARTFELT, accepting, seeking community? Some practical ideas will emerge as I tell the story of my first experience with the Alpha course, which does an excellent job of fostering seeking community. (Appendix four offers a brief overview of the Alpha course.)

Paula was a seeker. Her soul had been awakened, and she was interested in God but very distrustful toward the church. Her sister, Jamie, heard we were starting an Alpha course to provide community and a place for seekers to ask their questions. Jamie didn't even know her sister had started to seek a connection with God. Jamie thought first of her dad. But he wasn't interested. When Jamie mentioned the course to Paula, to Jamie's great surprise Paula expressed interest. So Jamie brought her to the banquet that kicks off the course.

The banquet started with great food and warm greetings. There was an energy and a wonderful sense of welcome and hospitality. Paula seemed to relax a little. Jamie introduced me to her, and I was able to thank her for coming and tell her how glad I was she could be there.

Over the meal we laughed and joked and avoided any spiritual conversation whatsoever. We talked about life and Chicago Bulls basketball, which during the Michael Jordan era was a very interesting subject to fellow Chicagoans.

After the meal, the emcee welcomed us and told a good joke on himself. We then went into a video: *Mr. Bean Goes to Church*. It was hilarious. And it absolutely roasted the church. At one point Mr. Bean has fallen asleep on the floor, precariously balanced on two knees. At another point he tries to join in singing "Alleluia," but all he knows is that one word. He mumbles through the song, only to belt it out every time he comes to an alleluia!

I then got up to speak on "Christianity: Boring, Untrue and Irrelevant?" I explained that church is often that way for me, but a genuine relationship with God is anything but. *That* is an adventure.

We invited people to join us to explore their spiritual longings and questions, and we announced when and where the Alpha course would start.

Paula really enjoyed herself; she liked all these people who were spiritually interested but honest and authentic about their struggles with churches and church-type people. So she joined us at the first Alpha meeting. We met in a home.

We started with a great meal and lots of laughter and getting to know each other's interests. Again, we avoided spiritual conversation intentionally. After the meal, a short familiar hymn ("Amazing Grace"), a completely botched joke and a short talk about Jesus, participants broke into small groups. During the very short worship time, we were careful to sing something familiar rather than an intimate chorus addressed directly to God; that would feel awkward for pre-Christians. Paula really liked the botched joke. If I could make a fool of myself, she knew she didn't have to be afraid of embarrassing herself. But the highlight of the meeting for Paula was the small group time.

Nearly every one in the group was pre-Christian, and the two Christians in the group had been trained not to give answers and sound spiritual. We got to know each other, asked a couple of questions arising from the talk and then talked about why we were checking out the Alpha course. The pre-Christians started to share their doubts and questions honestly. When

Melissa expressed her doubts and struggles, and said straight up that she wasn't sure she believed in this stuff, Paula got totally excited. All of a sudden the group became a group for her, asking her kinds of questions and not getting simple religious answers in return. The pre-Christians helped each other toward God by being able to express their distance from God and make the journey together. It was so moving to watch, and so surprising to the two of us who were Christians.

On the sixth week we all went on a retreat that focused on the work of the Holy Spirit. We had a blast, enjoying the hotel setting and doing some activities to build a sense of community and connection. Saturday night Paula had an experience of God's love and presence. Before then she had experienced God a couple of times, and that was what had turned her from apathy to curiosity to pursuit. Now she was being encountered by God and being drawn into a trust relationship with him.

She finished the Alpha course and brought her mom to the next one, which again started with a celebration and testimony banquet. Paula became an apprentice leader for that next course. Before the following course, she gave a very moving testimony of how she had become a Christian to our whole church, challenging members to bring their friends to the next Alpha. Her enthusiasm, though she was clearly a quiet person, was contagious and electric.

Two things stood out in her story. One, she experienced God for herself. That was decisive. Two, she had found a loving, accepting, honest community in the Alpha course, a community where pre-Christians could bring their questions, needs, dreams and struggles. Her life has been transformed, and many others have come to Alpha or brought their friends to Alpha because of her story and influence.

Here again are twin themes of postmodern conversion stories: authentic community and genuine God experiences.

Making It Happen

The Alpha training was great preparation for us to develop the kind of community pre-Christians would be attracted to and hang with.

What follow are practical suggestions for developing that kind of community, taken from our experience with Alpha and confirmed in visits to many other ministries that offer good community for postmodern people. These suggestions fit large meetings where you are trying to foster a sense of community, small group meetings such as groups investigating God (GIGs) and programs like Alpha where time is divided between large and small groups.

1. *Think through the experience of pre-Christian attendees from the time they leave their home, apartment or dorm room until the time they get back.* What would help them feel comfortable? Who ought to pick them up at their door? What familiar music could be playing as they enter your gathering? What kind of greeting would put them at ease? What would you like them to experience? How can you make a good first impression? First impressions are often lasting impressions.

2. *Designate greeters who are warm, look like the people you are trying to welcome, and are outgoing but not intrusive.* The greeters could hand people a program, which might just contain a word of welcome or might orient them to the event—this will help them relax because they know what's coming. If you're hosting a small group, you are the main greeter. But link them up with others in the group according to areas of common interest as soon as you can.

3. *Nametags help people know that this event is for new people, not just old-timers.* But don't force people to use them. And you won't need them for small groups.

4. *Create a space that is warm, is filled with light, has good energy and has familiar, upbeat music playing at low volume in the background.* If you are meeting in someone's home, gather in the warmest and most welcoming room. Have food and refreshments available. Don't underestimate the importance of pictures and prominently displayed books to help you set the tone. Not necessarily religious pictures and books, though.

5. *Start and end with social interaction over food or drink.* Seek to identify shared areas of interest, and avoid spiritual conversations early on. Many ministries I know offer Starbuck's coffee after their gatherings. Jesus knew the importance of food and festivity in reaching the people of his day. He spent more time at parties than at synagogues, at least if we can go by the evidence we have in the Gospels!

6. *The first person who speaks or opens the meeting needs to be warm, hospitable, comfortable and able to laugh at himself or herself.* The best thing I did at my first Alpha meeting was completely botch a good joke and then laugh at myself. Everybody relaxed and entered in at that point. Postmodern people are immediately drawn to Christians who are willing to look foolish!

7. *Avoid in-language, spiritual language and announcements for insiders only.* Nothing turns people off faster. I once visited a GIG and was introduced as a national "evangelist" to college students. Right off I was in a hole! The next announcement was about "DPMs." What are DPMs? No pre-Christian there had any idea! (FYI: daily prayer meetings!) To state it positively, use shared language and make mention of shared cultural experiences.

8. *In small groups, make sure there are more pre-Christians than Christians.* This one is critical! Teach the Christians to resist the temptation to give the answers, but help pre-Christians answer and talk to each other. This dynamic may be the most important, and it is toughest to pull off initially. Christians always seem to want to give answers early and often. At this state, shared questions are profoundly more helpful in establishing a community in which the Spirit can work.

9. *In discussions, get everyone sharing, and don't let anyone dominate.* It can really help to lay down some ground rules for everyone that challenge them to participate appropriately but that don't control what people say. Here's a suggestion for ground rules:

☐ I want you to enjoy yourself.

☐ I want you to listen to each other.

☐ I want you to grow, but I don't care how.

☐ I want you to be curious and to ask questions and express your ideas. Any honest question is appropriate.

☐ I want us to keep going back to the passage together and learning all we can from the wisdom Jesus has for our lives. That can keep us from going off on lots of tangents.

10. *Keep worship simple, heartfelt and understandable.* When possible, use songs that are familiar in the broader culture, like "Amazing Grace." Move into deeper intimacy with God as the weeks go on, but not at first. Here are some simple suggestions for worship with pre-Christians from Rick Warren's book *The Purpose Driven Church* (pp. 286-91).

☐ Preview all the music you use. Use the music that fits the purpose for your service. Choose music that fits the mood you want to create.

☐ Speed up the tempo.

☐ Update the lyrics. Use language unbelievers can understand. "Jehovah Jireh" might as well be "Mumbo Mugambo" to an unbeliever!

☐ Develop a hot worship band for large community-building gatherings.

☐ Don't force unbelievers to sing.

11. *Keep prayer simple, heartfelt and short.* Your goal is to get pre-Christians and new Christians praying, not to impress them with your prayer abilities. If someone goes on and on in prayer, pull them aside that very evening and explain the need for brevity. Prayer for one another can be a powerful experience. At Alpha, though, we wait until the retreat the fifth week. Prayer is intimate and takes lots of trust.

12. *Keep the message or Bible study humorous, spontaneous, chatty and intimate.* Postmodern people connect when we share our struggles and especially when we tell humorous stories on ourselves. Try never to preach at pre-Christian people; instead speak personally with passion and conviction.

13. Learn to have great parties and to sponsor events, like working at a food pantry, that build great community. A vibrant campus ministry at the University of Wisconsin-Madison starts the year with a mega-bonfire, a barn-dancing party to beat all barn-dancing parties, and a freshman celebration on State Street, the party strip of Madison.

14. *Train your leaders to work with you in pulling off these suggestions.* Again, the Alpha course training is fabulous for getting your leaders to think through community for pre-Christians. This book can also be helpful.

With these principles in mind, consider another outstanding model God is using today to draw pre-Christians into seeking community.

The Power of a GIG

As a sophomore in college, I rededicated my life to God. I began to pray for my friends. God laid Scott on my heart. I looked for opportunities to be with Scott. He liked to ski. So did I. Unfortunately, I had Christian activities scheduled when the ski club went skiing. So out went a few Christian activities. Sometimes to get to *real* Christian community that draws in pre-Christian people we need to cut out some of our endless Christian activities!

On the slopes with Scott, I totally botched starting a spiritual conversation. I felt humiliated and vowed never to try again. But we did have some great time to share some of our struggles and our experiences growing up.

On the last run, after I had given up all hope of conversation about spiritual things, Scott skied up to me and asked if I was involved in that fellowship group on campus, and whether we do anything with the Bible. I admitted we did. He then said he had been thinking about things and wondered if the Bible could help him in his life right now. He had never read it, so he had no idea where to start. Could I help him?

"Sure," I responded. That was the impressive contribution I made to my first evangelistic conversation.

At that point I began to practice team evangelism. I invited a friend who had been a Christian for ten years to look at the Bible with Scott and me. I needed the encouragement and accountability to keep taking the risks.

We met the next week, in Scott's room—I figured that he would have to show up if it was in his room. We studied in Genesis, looking at God as Creator.

At the end Scott piped up, "This is great, but how do I do it?"

"How do you do what?" I wanted to know.

"How do I get God in my life?"

"Well," I reflected, "you just get God in your life."

"But how?"

"Just do it!" I exclaimed.

"That's not helping, Rick."

Finally, in exasperation I blurted out, "That's study number *six*. We're on study number *one*. Can't you wait?"

Then wisely (and desperately) I turned to my teammate. "Any ideas, Kip?" He wasn't much better prepared for Scott's questions, but he did know enough to hand him a little booklet by John Stott, *Becoming a Christian*. Kip was as weak as I was! It's a good thing God was there!

The next day Scott called. "Rick, I did it."

"Fabulous, Scott. That's just great. I'm so happy for you. Uh, by the way, what did you do?"

Scott went on to explain how he had come into a relationship with Jesus. He taught *me* how to become a Christian!

You can see how much I helped my first "convert" to come to Jesus. That's team evangelism out of weakness. Can anybody say it was our cleverness and not God's power? No way!

Yet I did take the risk to relate, to build the friendship, to give verbal witness, to recruit a teammate. God's power was made perfect in our weakness. And to this day it encourages my faith, it renews genuine Christian experience in my life, to think about how God worked in my friendship with Scott.

Groups investigating God (GIGs) like the one I led are being used today by God in an exploding movement to reach pre-Christian people. If you take only one step forward in reaching people, start a GIG with the resources listed in appendixes two and three. Nothing could be more strategic and life-changing for you and your pre-Christian friends! You don't need a big church or group to start this kind of group. You don't need a worship leader. You don't need a stage or media equipment or money (though as you'll see, a VCR can help). You only need you and a pre-Christian friend. And you'll find that many of your friends will be interested.

You can plan meetings, print publicity, invite speakers, set up rooms, write dramas and produce outstanding media pieces without ever talking to a single pre-Christian person. But you can *never* pull off a GIG without talking to a pre-Christian friend about spiritual things and then getting into Scripture with her.

Evangelism is about helping people belong so that they come to believe. May God give us wisdom and courage to become more authentic, more Spirit-filled and more skilled at welcoming pre-Christian people into our Christian community.

Discussion Questions

1. Look over the guidelines for developing community that is attractive to pre-Christian people (pp. 113-16). Evaluate your evangelistic efforts according to these guidelines. What do you want to do, as an individual or a group, to grow in these skills?

2. Have you ever taken part in a GIG? What did you experience? What did you learn?

3. Would you consider starting a GIG? With whom? How could you get started? What help do you need? You can refer to appendixes two and three to figure out your next steps.

4. Are there other ways God is leading you to invite pre-Christians into seeking community (for example, worship, prayer, service, missions, road trips)? Brainstorm, making sure to apply the guidelines from pages 113-16 to each approach.

12

CONVERSION FOR
PRE-CHRISTIAN
PEOPLE TODAY

In general, people today will commit themselves to Christ in the context of community, a personal experience of God and a clear call to change allegiance. They need to ask Jesus to be at the center of their lives and to wrap their sense of identity around him. Later in this chapter we will look closely at the gospel message, considering a new emphasis for sharing the content of the good news. But first, a few comments about when and where we can call our friend to trust and commit herself to Christ.

Experience-oriented, community-seeking people today often genuinely trust Christ in weekend and week-long conferences. Soon I will be speaking at a seeker retreat in northern New York. More than two hundred people are expected, fifty of them seekers. The theme is "True Love 2000," and my wife and I will be sharing from our struggles the lessons we've learned about communication, commitment, healing and faith.

I have seen many seekers find Christ at these kinds of events, extended occasions to learn about and experience God and the Christian community.

In Alpha, described in the previous chapter, the majority of participants open their lives to Christ at the weekend retreat midway through the program, especially when the leaders conduct a time of teaching and ministry focused on the Holy Spirit. Appendix five outlines a sample seeker retreat for your use.

Once again, the experiential and community-focused dynamics are critical to conversion. We do not just make an appeal to the intellect at some large gathering, though that will help some people.

This chapter is more weighted in theology than the rest of the book. The material is valuable if you can work it through. If you find it too challenging or meaty, jump to the application-oriented chapter that follows.

Now let's look more deeply at the content of the message that God might use in an increasingly postmodern world.

The New Challenge

As I recounted earlier, I spent the summer after I graduated from college doing missions work in Southern Ireland with a group called Operation Mobilization. I was with a team of people from around the world. We were given a van, money for our first meal, instructions on how to trust God in prayer for all of our other meals, and a vanload of books to sell to people as we went door to door.

We visited most of the ten thousand people in that small town of Thurles in County Tipperary, made famous by the song: "It's a long way to Tipperary, it's a long way back home." We sold books, preached in the marketplace, held coffees, prayed all night once a week. As I talked to person after person, I felt as if I had entered a different world. Pre-Vatican II Catholicism was still alive and well and nearly all-powerful in that small community. Ninety-nine percent of the people were Roman Catholic.

One day we worshiped and then preached on a street corner. A man named Sean approached me and told me how much he admired our faith, even though he could never do what we were doing. I asked him why. He began to talk of his life and soon opened up about his experiences in the Irish Republican Army (IRA). He told me he had killed men and enjoyed it, because those men deserved it. He was full of a passion for justice, and also hatred for those he thought had been unjust.

I had a chance that afternoon to walk Sean through a gospel outline called "The Bridge." I was amazed at how deeply Sean resonated with what

I said. He knew God had created the world. He knew God was a just judge. He knew all people deserved death for their sins, though he felt the sins of some (the unjust occupiers of Northern Ireland) were greater than others'. By the time I began to speak of Jesus' death, he was crying out for what could answer the problem of his guilt before God. He was hopeful that Jesus' death could be the answer, though he had never understood God loved him like that. When we parted, he was seriously considering committing his life to Jesus.

I recently had another very different experience. I shared the same Bridge diagram with a young woman at a nearby college. The response was very different. She hadn't thought much about God's creating the world. She had a very eclectic notion of God, patterned more on the idea of the Force in Star Wars than the biblical personal God of creation. She couldn't imagine God being angry about her sin; she couldn't conceive of her sin as that serious. And the idea that God would kill his own Son was scandalous to her.

Needless to say, she did not leave ready to commit her life to Jesus, though she was happy for me, that I had found something that seemed to be working in my life. "It just doesn't float my boat" were her parting words.

I've thought a lot about the contrast between these two people. Martin Luther lived at the dawn of the modern world. He was haunted by the question, How can I, a sinner, find acceptance from a holy God? His question rang true biblically, and it also rang true for his generation. No longer could the church be the mediator between the individual and God. The modern mindset opposed tradition and valued the autonomy of the individual before God. But what was the individual to do in his personal spiritual struggle to deal with deepening guilt and alienation from God as he faced a new sense of individual and moral responsibility? What was the new modern to do with his growing sense of conscience?

Luther was also God-centered. His other great question was, How can God embrace sinners and still be just and holy? Luther struggled with understanding how God could answer God's own dilemma of conscience.

Luther found his answer—and a powerful answer it was for the emerging modern consciousness—in his rediscovery of the centrality of justification by faith. God, the just Judge of the autonomous individual, had poured out his anger at sin on Jesus at the cross. He had declared Jesus the righteous guilty, so he could now declare the guilty righteous. The penalty had been paid. The individual could now know he was loved, could relate to God as an individual and could turn to the Bible as the ground of his personal life of conscience. And God could embrace the sinner and still be holy and just. God's conscience was clear and God's integrity intact.

Here is how Luther expressed his modern approach to faith and conscience:

> Unless I am convinced by Scripture and plain reason—I do not accept the authority of popes and councils, for they have contradicted each other—my conscience is captive to the Word of God. I cannot and I will not recant anything, for to go against conscience is neither right nor safe. God help me. Amen. (quoted by Tarnas, p. 239)

The modern worldview superseded the medieval worldview, but the Christian could assume some common knowledge of that medieval Christian world view when telling the gospel message to a rational, analytical modernist person. That's what I found in Ireland. Luther's formulation of the gospel was powerful, liberating, resonant for nearly everyone I talked to. Luther's question was their question. Luther's rediscovery of justification by faith was as rebellious and freeing an act for them in their experience of the church as it had been for Luther himself. I began to grasp how powerfully Luther's proclamation would have rung throughout the length and breadth of Germany, amidst growing individualism, economic freedom and rising nationalism. Even in the 1970s, that age of intermixed modern and medieval was alive and well in this southern Irish town.

In our postmodern culture we cannot assume what I could assume in Southern Ireland. We cannot assume people are familiar with Scripture or basic biblical ideas. We cannot assume that they feel accountable in any way to a supreme being. We cannot assume that they feel much real guilt for sin. We cannot assume that they even think at all in terms of sin. We cannot assume that they will need to have any logical consistency or coherence to their ideas about God. After all, the postmodern assumption is that we create our own reality in the arena of spirituality. In a biblically illiterate, subject-centered postmodern world we face new challenges to communicate the gospel in a meaningful, true and resonant way.

With this in mind, let's look at the content of the gospel and recover some often neglected truths that can make our sharing of the gospel more compelling for postmodern people.

Recovering Theological Truths

Using 1 Corinthians 15, we can summarize the facts of the gospel as C. H. Dodd did some years ago (Dodd, p. 13).

1. Prophecies are fulfilled. The new age has been inaugurated. The Messiah has come.

2. He was born of the seed of David.

3. He died according to the Scriptures, to deliver us out of the present evil age.

4. He was buried.

5. He rose on the third day according to the Scriptures.

6. He is exalted at the right hand of God and has poured out God's Spirit.

7. He will come again to judge the living and the dead.

But what do these facts mean? How do they operate to give us salvation? How do we interpret these truths?

For the last forty years a profound discussion has been going on in the church regarding the nature of the gospel, particularly in relation to the meaning of the death of Jesus on the cross. In a little book called *Christus Victor* Gustaf Aulén, a Swedish systematic theologian, compares and contrasts three different views. I have adapted Aulén's views to fit my purpose in this chapter.

First, Aulén points to the *satisfaction* theory of the atonement, originated by Anselm in his famous book in the twelfth century, *Cur Deus Homo (Why God Became Man)*. Here Anselm first fully developed the idea that salvation was an objective work in which God reconciles human beings to himself by pouring out his wrath on Jesus, thus satisfying his own justice and simultaneously accepting human beings. God could be just and still justify the unjust. Salvation was first of all a change in God, a way for God to remain holy and yet become one with sinners he loves. This idea of salvation and of Jesus' death is the idea that the bridge diagram captures. Since Luther's time, evangelicals have taken this as the key idea for a non-Christian to accept in order to cross the line of faith and become a Christian.

The second idea about Jesus' death that Aulén points to was first fully developed by Abelard in the twelfth century: that Jesus is an *example* for us. By his sacrificial death Jesus makes his appeal to us to change and choose to be reconciled to God. Jesus' death operates for us like the death of Gandhi or the death of Martin Luther King Jr. It is an appeal to our hearts, our highest selves, to live as they lived. Thus the key change is not in God but in us. In that way this theory of Jesus' death is *subjective*. The satisfaction theory, which assumes that the change is brought about by God and takes place first within God, has been called the *objective* view of salvation. The conflict between liberal theology and conservative theology has often been a battle between these two theories of how Jesus' death works to bring salvation.

Aulén goes on to suggest a third view of the meaning of Jesus' death. He traced its beginning to the early church fathers of the second century, and through them back to the Scriptures. Aulén calls this the *classical* view of the atonement. In this view Jesus' death was a victory over the evil powers of this world and the spiritual powers in the heavens, powers that had people in bondage, the powers of sin and Satan and death. Jesus' death took away their power over us, freeing us to serve and love God. We desperately need to recover this theme as we share the gospel today. Key elements of this understanding are as follows:

1. *Adam and Eve chose to be ruled by sin, Satan and death* when they chose to disobey God. Sin, Satan and death are rightful rulers over human beings, because people choose to give their allegiance to other things rather than to God. Adam and Eve represent all of us in their choice, and their choice has affected all of us. But we also choose just as they did to replace God with other things at the center of our lives. We think we can control those other things, but they end up controlling us. God's wrath is expressed in that God gives us up to the consequences of our choices. *Left to ourselves we face an eternity of slavery, aloneness and misery, subject to sin, Satan and death.*

2. But God didn't leave us there. He sent his Son. Jesus was the new man. *Jesus redid, or recapitulated, the life of Adam, this time choosing to obey God, live with God at the center,* and reject all those other things that want to replace God and take our allegiance. In his life Jesus bound the strong man, Satan, and took his goods, the lives and allegiance of men and women (see Mk 3:27).

3. Jesus' obedience took him to the cross. *On the cross Jesus exposed and unmasked sin, Satan, and death for what they are.* They are gibbering, destructive, hateful things that consume and kill their victims mercilessly.

4. *On the cross Jesus took all hatred, destruction, woundedness, shame and death onto himself.* All the judgment and power and hatred Satan had the right to pour out on humankind, because humans had chosen to follow

Satan, was now poured out on the one man who was innocent and over whom Satan had no rightful power. The innocent died for the guilty, in the place of the guilty. *And Satan lost his legitimacy, his right to judge. On the cross Satan was unmasked, and his power and right to rule lost their legitimacy.*

5. *Because Jesus was innocent, God raised him from the dead,* for death had no real power or real right over him.

6. *Now we can all choose to identify with Jesus, to give him our allegiance.* Jesus' life and obedience become our life and obedience. Jesus' death becomes our death. *Satan no longer has any right to us. Sin no longer has the right to rule us.* Jesus' resurrection will become our resurrection, the first-fruits of which we have received in the gift of the Spirit. In the life of the Spirit the new age of God's rule is already operating. It will not be completely fulfilled until Jesus comes again, but we can experience significant liberation now.

Colossians 2:13-15 offers a Christus Victor picture of the meaning of Jesus' death.

> When you were dead in your sins and in the uncircumcision of your sinful nature, God made you alive with Christ. He forgave us all our sins, having canceled the written code, with its regulations, that was against us and that stood opposed to us; he took it away, nailing it to the cross. And having disarmed the powers and authorities, he made a public spectacle of them, triumphing over them by the cross.

In C. S. Lewis's *The Lion, the Witch and the Wardrobe* the lion Aslan, a Christ-figure, is killed by the White Witch, who has the right to a kill for a boy named Edmund. Edmund had betrayed his brother and sisters and given his allegiance to the White Witch. Aslan approaches the hill of the Stone Table where the execution will take place, accompanied by two sisters, Lucy and Susan. They watch from a hedge as Aslan goes to the hill and is attacked by a gibbering, destructive, craven crowd of goblins, ghouls and hags. He is killed, the innocent for the guilty. But there is a deeper law at work. Death begins to work backwards. The White Witch loses her right to judge and her power to kill. She ends up dead. Aslan ends up more alive than ever. Edmund ends up free.

Whom Will We Worship?

This understanding of salvation sees humans caught between competing loyalties. The key issue is idolatry. Whom do you worship? Humans were made to worship. We will worship something or someone, whether God, other gods, the law, created things, other men or other women, sexuality, science, technology, our own rational mind, our cultural background or identity, our consciousness or ourselves. Humans will worship. Sin at its heart is idolatry, not acknowledging God as God but worshiping created things instead of God. Once we choose to worship other things in the place of God, our understanding becomes darkened and our lives become confused. We enter into all kinds of sin—sexual, relational, rational, occult. We are in bondage. We are ruled by the power of these other gods over our lives.

And these other gods have a reality beyond just their material reality. Money is material, but it is also spiritual, as Jesus clearly taught in his words about Mammon. Sex is physical, but it is also spiritual. We need only consider ancient fertility cults and the worship of Baal and Ashtoreth. Every god we worship, every thing we put in the place of God, has these several dimensions of reality. They become our idols. They become our personal demons. Many of them have become our society's demons. They rule our lives. In the case of sex and alcohol, they can become powerful addictions, exerting their rule in our lives in horrifying and destructive ways. In the case of nationalism and tribalism, they can become the source of an almost demonic hatred that we see played out graphically in the racism of our society and ethnic cleansing in other societies.

Such evil is not just personal and rational. It is somehow transcendent and irrational as well. A gospel that merely addresses an individual's personal guilt and has no answer to the addictions and evil and bondage of our day will seem irrelevant and reductionistic. In the end such a gospel will not be taken seriously in our postmodern world.

The modern worldview saw belief in Satan and the powers and principalities as primitive and outmoded. In a postmodern world, interest in the spiritual world, in angels and devils, in magic, the occult, and fantasy has mushroomed. People today can see themselves as pawns of powers that are bigger than they are. They look to the spiritual world for meaning and help. Shows and books and articles on angels have multiplied. Jesus' victory over darkness and Jesus' deliverance from the power of addiction are dimensions of the good news whose relevance has returned with intensity.

My conviction is that all three dimensions of the atonement—Jesus' satisfaction of God's righteous anger against sin; Jesus' victory over the power of sin, Satan and death; and Jesus' appeal of love to our hearts—are true and important ways to see the death of Jesus. But the point of contact—that point at which the gospel first floods a person with the light of God's love and power and ushers the person toward the center of faith—is changing. The understanding of Jesus' death as a victory, a release of the slaves of sin, Satan and death, is as relevant and resonant a point of entry into salvation for the postmodern as the view of Jesus' death as a satisfaction of God's just anger against sin. Both must ultimately be understood and embraced if a truly Christian faith is to be developed. And when all three views are held together, we have a much fuller biblical picture of the gospel of the kingdom that weaves through all of the New Testament.

But the entry point, the point of contact and trust and initial commitment, is shifting to include this idea of liberation. And that shift is good. It is a recovery of the way the gospel was most often proclaimed to unbelievers through the first millennium of the history of the church.

Justification by faith was the key issue for the materialistic modern person seeking acceptance from a just God in the context of a legalistic and corrupt church. It was the key way to understand salvation in light of God's struggle with his own holy dilemma, loving the sinner and hating the sin. And it was the key idea Paul developed to answer Jewish critics of his mission to the Gentiles. It is still, of course, an absolutely critical idea, and a key part of receiving the salvation that God alone can give.

But deliverance from the rule of the powers of the flesh, the world and the devil into the rule of God is also a critical dimension of the gospel for a postmodern to hear. The experiential, community-seeking, spiritually "creative" postmodern person has returned to a mindset that is in many ways close to the mindset of the pagans to whom the gospel was first proclaimed.

The Christus Victor understanding of Jesus' death on the cross has often served as the central gateway into salvation in pagan contexts, and it still does in many missionary situations today. Often the key crisis in a premodern culture is the power encounter, in which God proves victor over the forces and spirits that rule a people. I am more and more convinced that this understanding of Christ's victory on the cross and his power over the enslaving, addictive powers in our day will also be a decisive dimension for many postmodern people.

We are in a time of transition. A faithful proclamation of the gospel today must bring together these themes. So let us turn to a gospel presentation that God has been using powerfully with experiential, community-seeking people. It integrates the three significant understandings of the meaning of the death of Christ. It speaks to people's needs for experiential truth, help with their sense of identity and self, and need for symbols and pictures to capture their imagination.

The outline emphasizes the cross and the resurrection powerfully and appropriately and in a God-centered way, but it also does things that some other outlines don't do very well. It starts with creation, where many biblically illiterate people need to start today. It defines sin as idolatry in a way that is biblical *and* makes convicting sense to people today. And it emphasizes union with Christ as the goal of repentance and faith. We don't just "cross a bridge" to be with God, as one popular outline has it. We actually invite God to make his home in us, at the center of who we are, by the operation of his Holy Spirit.

I present the outline in the context of my own story and my own conversion. My hope is that you can learn to tell your own story using this gospel presentation. You will find that you can draw the simple pictures on a napkin, if need be! Thus in the next chapter I tell my story, and at the end you will find a boiled-down summary of the outline for your understanding, adaptation and use, both for yourself and for training others.

It has been very exciting to see people today responding to Jesus as I and many others have used this presentation. It is available as a booklet titled *Circles of Belonging.* May God bless you as you share the good news!

Discussion Questions

1. What do you think about the author's argument that the victory of Christ on the cross over sin, Satan and death is a very important theme for us to recover as we share the good news with people today?

2. Look at Colossians 2:13-15. How would you summarize the content of the gospel from this passage?

3. How does this understanding of Christ's victory on the cross and our liberation help us lead people naturally into Christian growth and discipleship after they respond to the gospel?

13

INVITING PEOPLE INTO THE CIRCLE OF BELONGING

WHO AM I? WHERE DO I BELONG? WHERE WILL I FIND LOVE? HAVE YOU EVER asked yourself these questions? I know I have. Often.

In my last year in high school I was consumed by those questions. It started on a bus ride, a ski trip to northern Pennsylvania with my high-school ski club. Several rows from the back seat of the bus, where I liked to hang out, I saw a cascade of blond hair falling over the back of a seat. I thought, *That looks intriguing.* So I decided to make my way forward to join John, my friend who liked to hang out in the front seat of the bus.

I neglected to think up anything to say to John. So I felt a little foolish as our conversation stalled. But I quickly forgot my embarrassment as I went back to my seat. Yes! That cascade of blond hair was definitely intriguing! *Maybe I'll run into her out on the slopes,* I hoped.

On my third time down, as I stood at the bottom of the run, I looked up the slope to see a person hurtling in my general direction, blond hair streaming behind. She flashed by me and collided with a nearby woman. I hurried over. Concerned about both victims of the wipeout, I asked Blond Hair if she was OK. "Yes, I'm fine," she responded. I helped her up.

"My name is Rick."

"My name is Karen."

And we were on our way! The next time down we skied together. Half-way down, I waited. There she came again, hurtling down the slope, blond hair streaming. Again she flashed by me, and this time she collided with a young man.

Concerned about both of the tumblers, once again I skied over to Karen, helped her up, asked her if she was OK. "Yes, I'm fine!" And off we went again.

At the bottom of the hill I waited for her. This time when she flew past me there was no one to "catch" her. I winced as she came to a full and ungraceful stop against the big picture window of the lodge, those inside looking out at her with alarm and wonder in their eyes.

"Karen, I'm noticing a pattern. You seem to get along well until it comes to the stopping part, and then things seem to get fairly dramatic."

"Yeah, nobody ever taught me how to stop these things!" she responded, looking down at her skis.

"I'd be glad to help." So I taught her to shush and snowplow and stop—to the great delight of everyone who had had the opportunity of becoming acquainted with Karen on the slopes!

At the end of the evening I asked Karen out. I had to ask several times over the next several evenings, because she had just broken up with someone, but she finally agreed. Little did I know that sailing along fine followed by crash-and-burn endings on the slopes was a pattern that would also come to characterize our relationship. Had I known, I would have helped the other hapless tumblers and let Karen fend for herself.

We just never seemed to be able to communicate well. And I will never forget the prom night from hell. We did fine until midnight. But somehow, when it came to the kissing part, she got upset about something I'd done, blew me off and got another ride home.

Two weeks later the inevitable happened. She told me she didn't want to date anymore. Then she let me know she had never really been attracted to me and that it had been a mistake to ever go out. This was after six months of fairly intense dating.

Flight from Rejection

Have you ever felt rejection like that? It stays in the pit of your stomach, sometimes for months. That experience brought out all my loneliness, all my longing for acceptance and belonging, all my need to feel good about who I was and how I looked.

Many of us have those needs and longings. We want to know we're accepted for who we are, that someone thinks we're special and attractive. We want to feel at home with ourselves and at least a few other people.

Some of us grew up in families that fell apart. Some of us grew up in families that never really grew together. In my family it was very hard to express affection, to ask for what I needed, to trust that I was known and loved for who I was. Maybe it was that way in your family too.

After the breakup with Karen, I went into a shell and built a wall around myself. But I still needed to feel loved, to belong. So starting midway through my freshman year in college, I began a series of dating relationships that were my attempt to find love, acceptance and belonging.

During that next three years of college, I had to be dating at all times. If I didn't have someone to go out with, I knew that I would be unhappy, that I would have to face what I was feeling. I didn't want to do that. So I filled my time with relationships and with escape. I escaped into fantasy (go Trekkies!) and constant music. I escaped into the parties at my Sigma Chi fraternity house. And I was always starting a new relationship as soon as the old one ended. Sometimes in very awkward ways, the beginning of a new relationship overlapped with the ending of the old one.

Then, in the midst of my search for identity, belonging and love, I ran into Jim in the student union. He was working at a Christian booktable, engaging seeking people in spiritual conversations. I thought, *I eat Christians for lunch. I can ask a few devastating questions, and Jim will probably lose his faith.* So I gave him my best questions. How can a loving God send people to hell? How can an all-powerful God stand by and let so many innocent people suffer in the world? Why are some Christians so hypocritical? Why are they so narrow, uptight and judgmental toward other people? Why are they against premarital sex and homosexuality and people's freedom and fun?

Always before, well-meaning people had told me that I just had to have faith. Well, I didn't have faith, so their answer never did me any good. But Jim didn't respond that way. He had thoughtful answers to my questions.

He admitted when he didn't know something. He seemed to be taking me seriously. I felt listened to and cared for. And my heart began to open up.

As I watched Jim, he seemed to know who he was. He seemed to feel a sense of belonging wherever he went, and he gave other people that sense. He was at home with himself, and I felt more at home with myself when I was around him. So I began asking him questions. He told me he had found a life-changing relationship with God. Did I want that too?

I wasn't even sure what he was talking about. So he asked if I wanted to hear a brief summary of the message of the Christian faith. He asked if he could show me a picture of how I could find out who I was and where I belonged through a relationship with God.

"OK," I responded, though I was feeling awkward.

What Jim shared with me I now share with you. Over the years I've adapted it to make it clearer and more helpful. Hopefully this graphic summary of God's message to us, found in the Bible, will help you as much as it did me.

*   *   *   *

The Circle of Belonging: A Simple Way to Explain the Good News of Jesus

At first, all creation was in the circle of belonging.

God made the world. God made you—to love God, to be loved by God. We were made to have God at our center and through God to know we are God's children. With God in the center, we were in right relationship with ourselves and everything else.

Do you long to belong, to know who you are, to know you matter and are deeply and passionately loved by the God who made you? I know I wanted that. So what has happened? Why do we feel so alone, so distant from God?

We loved other things more than God, resulting in spiritual death.

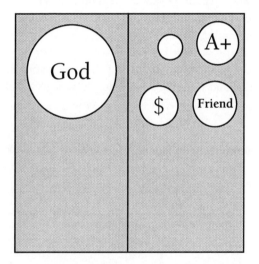

Unfortunately, we choose to substitute something else for God at the center of our lives. Maybe a boyfriend or girlfriend. Maybe a family or culture. Maybe achievement or performance. Maybe a role we play. Maybe our sexuality or gender, or approval from our parents or acceptance from our circle of friends. We forget that we are much more than any of these things.

Substituting something else for God at the center of our lives is what the Bible calls sin. And we all sin. We try to run our own lives, we try to create our own identity. We wrap our identity up in these other things, but they can't deliver and they will always disappoint us. Our lives become more fragmented, more painful, more scattered. At the center of our lives, where God should be, we experience an emptiness.

I was seeking to wrap my life up in relationships and experiences. If I could only find the right girl, or experience the best high, I would feel better about life. I would discover who I really was. But it wasn't working. I still felt empty and often alone. How are you seeking to fill that emptiness and aloneness? Is it working for you?

In the Bible God tells us that as we reject God in favor of other things, we hurt ourselves, others and God. God hates our choice to replace God with other things. Without God in the center, our identity, our view of ourselves and our relationships with others are distorted. We often feel ashamed of who we are. We end up alone and disconnected. The lack of God at the center of our lives results in spiritual death. If we never turn toward God, that aloneness and emptiness and shame and spiritual death lasts forever! The Bible calls this condition hell.

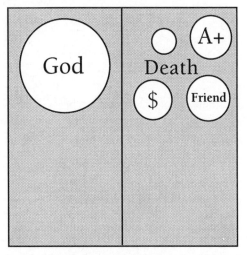

To me this sounded harsh. Yet it made sense too. I knew I needed something more at the center of who I was. I was starting to want God back in the center. But how could that happen? What could I do?

Jesus died for us, taking on the death we deserve.

Fortunately, God didn't leave us alone and spiritually dead. Out of passionate love for us, God wants to be restored as the center. God wants us to live in our identity as a loved child of God. So God came to us as a human being, Jesus.

Jesus was God. Jesus created love and acceptance and belonging wherever he went because God was his center. He showed people who they really were, and he showed people how to live with all those other things in right relationship with the real center.

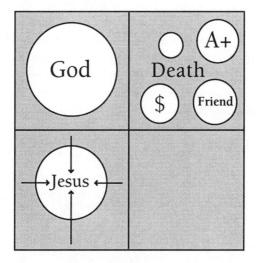

And then, even though God was his center, he died for us. He was killed on the cross, taking on all the consequences of our choice to run our own lives and to live with other things at the center. At the cross Jesus took on himself the spiritual death we deserved.

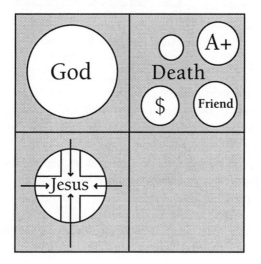

Jesus offers us a way back into the circle of belonging.

What's more, Jesus didn't just die. He came back from death, and he is alive today. The evidence that Jesus rose from death is astonishing. He *is* alive! So he can live in us, at our center, restoring God to the central place in our lives. Jesus will forgive us for the pain we've caused and change us from the inside out. Jesus can give us the sense of belonging and identity we seek and restore right relationships with others and the rest of creation. We can live in our identity as God's child, part of God's family.

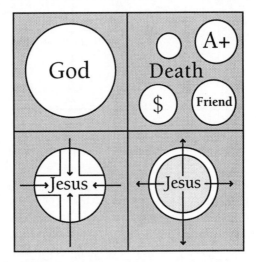

How does this happen?

☐ We *admit* our false centers and turn from them toward God.

☐ We *accept* Jesus' death for the death we deserve and the hurt we have caused.

☐ We *ask* Jesus to come into the center of our lives, and we *commit* ourselves to him as our forgiver, healer and leader. Through Jesus our real identity—God's beloved child—is reestablished in relationship with God.

Is God at the center of your life? Or is God somewhere else in your life, or even completely outside the circle of your life?

Asking Jesus into the center of your life is like a marriage commitment, like adoption into a new family. You don't understand all that you are committing yourself to when you start, but you know it will affect everything else in your life for the rest of your life!

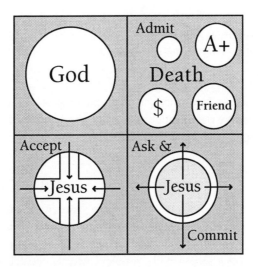

There were aspects of my dating relationships, intense and often satisfying emotional and physical experiences, that I didn't want to give up. I knew Jesus would have something to say about those parts of my life. But I also knew that I wanted and needed something more at the center of my life. I needed a relationship with God.

Do you want that?

It has been years now since I committed my life to God, and I have never regretted it. God is at the center of my life. That gives me a sense of fulfillment and hope. And it has put all the other relationships in better perspective. I am no longer alone at the center of who I am. The God who made me has now made his home in me, and I have never been the same. I am now experiencing life as God's child, as part of God's family.

You can pray a simple prayer to God as I did, and begin your new life with God at the center of who you are!

A Simple Prayer to Invite God into the Center of Your Life

Thank you, God, that you made me to know you and love you, to find love and belonging in a relationship with you at the center of my life, to be your beloved child.

I *admit* that I have replaced you at the center with other things and people, specifically *[in your own words, tell God what you have put before God in your life]*. I have hurt you and others, and I choose now to turn from those things at the center of my life back to you, God.

I *accept* that Jesus on the cross took on himself my sin of putting other things before you, God, and that he took on my spiritual death. And I thank you that you loved me so much that you sent your Son to live and die for me.

I now *ask* you, Jesus, to come into the center of my life, and I *commit* myself to you as my forgiver, healer and leader. Thank you that you restore my relationship with God and others, and that you will now change me from the inside out! Thank you, Jesus!

Helping You Get Started

If you have made this commitment and asked Jesus to come into the center of your life, you're now beginning the greatest adventure there is: growing your life with God. God will change you from the inside out. God will give you strength and wisdom to have new priorities and to relate to people in new ways. God is with you all the way, and actually lives inside you by the gift of the Holy Spirit. Rejoice! You are now living in the reality of being a beloved child of God.

How do you grow your life with God? Here again is the picture of life with Jesus at the center. The arrows point to the key ways you can grow your life with God.

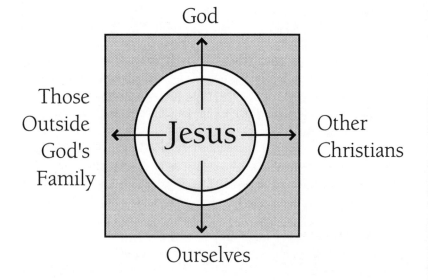

The upward arrow points toward your direct, conversational relationship with God. You can nurture that by spending time each day reading the Bible and then talking to God. When you read the Bible, you can start with a Gospel account of Jesus, say, the Gospel of John. Or you can use the Bible studies provided in appendix three. When you talk to God, use simple language. Speak praise for God's beauty, tenderness and power, give thanks for what God has done, and then bring your life before God and make your requests for the day. Make sure to spend a few moments quietly listening for any direction or encouragement God may want to give you. As you listen, you will sometimes have a sense in your heart of something God wants to say to you about your life or about the Scripture you have just read. Start praying and listening to God and reading the Bible for at least fifteen minutes a day.

Back to the drawing: One sideways arrow represents your relationships with other Christians. Your life with God won't grow unless you spend time with others in God's family, being encouraged, getting wisdom, asking for their prayers and just hanging out.

The other sideways arrow points toward others who are not yet in God's family. They need Jesus at the center of their lives too, and we get the privilege of telling them what God has done for us. Begin by sharing with a friend who doesn't know Jesus a few simple words on what God has just done in your life.

The downward arrow represents your relationship with yourself, your sexuality, your culture and your place in your family. God will begin to heal and restore you in these parts of your life. You can now trust God for new attitudes, new confidence to become who God made you to be.

God loves you. You were made for belonging and identity with God at the center of your life. God is with you and lives inside you by the Holy Spirit. Grow your life with God! It is the most extraordinary and transforming adventure there is.

If you've made this commitment, please let me know at <Rick_Richardson@ivstaff.org>. To be honest, your courageous choice will encourage me a lot! And I'd like to pray for you as you begin this great adventure.

Discussion Questions

1. Think through and tell your own conversion story, using the author's story at the beginning of this chapter as a model. What was at the center of your life

14

TRANSFORMATION
Getting & Growing a True Christian Identity

YES! OUR FRIEND HAS COME INTO THE KINGDOM. HE HAS ASKED JESUS TO BE at the center of his life, and he has turned away from the other centers from which he had sought to get his identity. He is starting to know himself as a beloved child of God. Now how do we help him be transformed in his identity? How do we help him walk into full freedom from the kinds of idolatry that have enslaved him? How do we help him become more like Jesus?

Our modernist mindset on discipleship would direct us to focus on our friend's mind and will. We might meet with him one on one and help him learn to study the Bible. We would teach him to have a quiet time, to study the Bible every day, to pray, to keep a list of his prayer requests so he can see which ones God answers and then give thanks. We would encourage our friend to be in Christian fellowship. After all, there are no lone ranger Christians, despite what our individualistic modernist culture might have pushed us toward. Finally, we would encourage him to share his faith with his friends. We would also listen to his struggles and encourage him to confess any sins to God, to get up again and go on, to know that God can always forgive him and he can always begin again with the slate wiped clean.

These activities are good. They can help our friend become a better follower of Jesus. I encouraged them in the last chapter as a great way to start with Christ. But they are often not enough, especially in a postmodern culture, to foster transformation. Our friend faces barriers, internal and external, that need to be addressed and dealt with if he is to experience transformation. Our discipleship process must adequately speak to the heart and the mind, to the body and the soul. It must call forth moral effort, but it must also provide power to overcome addictive patterns and healing to deal with debilitating wounds. It must speak to the core identity issues of the new believer.

Too often new believers have remained locked in addictive patterns of substance abuse, heterosexual or homosexual struggle, pornography, materialism and greed, anger, depression. Too often new believers have lived under the power of past hurts from abuse or divorce or tragedy or racism or sexism. If people cannot experience transformation in these dimensions of their lives, do we really have good news for our postmodern world? Do we have a message for which our enthusiasm can be sustained?

The Transformation of Postmodern Believers

Ten years ago I joined a small group that changed my life. It brought me into a new and ongoing experience of transformation. It helped me recover missing themes of transformation that were profoundly biblical and yet had been disturbingly absent from my Christian life. Our small group had three key mentors for recovering these missing dimensions of Christian transformation: Paul the apostle, C. S. Lewis the Cambridge professor, and Leanne Payne the writer and teacher on prayer and healing. Payne in particular has done seminal work in integrating Paul's theology of the "new person" in Christ with Lewis's insights into our true and false selves, or identities. She has applied these insights in a healing ministry that has provided great help to homosexual strugglers especially, but to many others of us as well. Her coworker Mario Bergner, a former homosexual struggler, has also been profoundly helpful in my process of transformation.

In a postmodern view, identity is developed through dialogue and community. But merely self- or socially-generated identity is profoundly insecure, particularly in a time of major fragmentation and loss of any secure basis for truth or value, such as we face in our culture. The person in a postmodern world cries out in anguish and anxiety to know who she is and to know that she matters. She often feels herself to be on a futile and conflicted search for a secure sense of self.

But in Christ we are a new creation! Our identity is certainly developed and expressed in dialogue and community with God and others. But our identity is also *given* us in some sense. We are re-created in union with Christ.

According to Paul, we got a new self—our true identity—through our union with Christ. God made his home in us. We are God's new temple, individually and corporately. When the Spirit took up residence in us, God made union with us (Eph 4:17—5:20).

Questions of Identity

As Leanne Payne has put it, "Another lives in us" (p. 21). That is the secret of the Christian life. At the heart of who we are as Christians is a new being, a new creation, produced by the union of God's Spirit with our spirit. This new creation is the determining fact of our existence and the basic ground of our identity. We get it as a gift. Now we need to become as adults what we already are in infancy. The life energy is there. The new identity is there. We merely need to choose to see it, to embrace it, to live in the reality of what we already are and have already been given.

Of course it takes all of our effort and lots of healthy community and dialogue with God and others to live in that reality. The false identities within us get so much attention and nurture from the world around us and from the prince of this world system, the devil.

When I work with Christians seeking transformation, I ask in whom or in what is this person attempting to gain his or her identity (Payne, p. 52). From what person or thing is he or she demanding, "Tell me who I am"? What is he or she bent toward? What does he or she seem constantly anxious about? I then know what the person's idol is, what "affections" need either to be renounced or to be set in perspective.

We are called as Christians to repent of sin, renounce idols, and ask God to redeem and set in order the genuine human needs that have become distorted and misdirected. I believe we have so focused on sin and repenting of sin as the key to transformation that we have missed other vital dimensions. We are right to turn away from sin, which is our choice to go our own way rather than

God's. But equally important, we must *renounce* idolatries and false identities. We haven't understood how critical this practice is for the health of the Christian life and the fashioning of a true identity. We are not to reject the genuine and God-given needs that lie behind many of our idolatries. We ask God to redeem them, to set in order those needs, so that worship of God is always primary and preeminent, and so that those needs are expressed and met in ways that fit our God-given identity rather than destroying it.

Personhood, identity, being itself comes from God, as our hands and hearts are open to receive and respond in obedience. Focused on God and listening to the words he speaks, we are freed from the lies that we are told by others, by our own unhealed hearts and by the devil (Payne, p. 53).

God wants to replace the false words with the truth about who you are. You are in his image. You are becoming like his Son. You are beloved. You are a glorious creature in the making. Lewis described you and me in his essay "The Weight of Glory".

> It is a serious thing to live in a society of possible gods and goddesses, and to remember that the dullest and most uninteresting person you can talk to may [be becoming] a creature which, if you saw it now, you would be strongly tempted to worship, or else a horror and a corruption such as you meet, if at all, only in a nightmare. All day long we are, in some degree, helping each other to one or other of these destinations. (Lewis, p. 18)

False identities are just as ultimately unreal and insubstantial as true identities are eternal and substantial. As one example, the homosexual identity is a false identity, woven around a self God neither created nor redeemed. In the end it won't exist. It is not your true self.

So how do we practice and help others into this oft-neglected key to transformation, this renouncing and utterly forsaking the "bent" posture toward the creature and "straightening" up into Christ and our true identity in Christ?

The Ministry of Transformation

Our traditional methods of discipleship are often failing us in regard to people's sexual, relational and gender identity struggles, and people are feeling trapped instead of transformed. The apostle Paul taught about sexual immorality as idolatry, and so this arena of our lives can especially be dealt with and helped in relation to Paul's teaching on idolatry and our true identity.

First, let's look at some of the biblical teaching on men, women, sexuality and idolatry. It is from the Bible that we learn what is our true identity as men and women.

Genesis 1—3 carries profound teaching on men and women. The curse in Genesis 3 is especially insightful about the idolatrous tendencies that are characteristic of men and women.

Men are told they will work by the sweat of their brow. Men are frustrated in their life of work, never finding the fulfillment and fruitfulness that they were made to experience. Thus men tend to be bent toward their work. They are also bent toward the approval of other men, especially their fathers. Ultimately this frustrated need has its root in the fall from favor with their heavenly Father. Unaffirmed men are unable to affirm other men. Unaffirmed fathers are unable to affirm their sons. And so the cycle goes on, down through generations. Men tend to wrap their identity up in their work and in the approval of other men. In an extreme form, this need for the approval of other men, and ultimately of their fathers, can lead to workaholism in one man and homosexuality in another.

Men in our culture have also experienced a loss of mothering. As a result, men can also be bent toward women, toward sex and pornography. Casual sex and pornography are the false, ultimately unsatisfying and addictive ways of connecting to the feminine need for nurture, for well-being and even for being itself. For men and women receive their initial life, well-being and sense of being from their mothers.

Male idolatry is often visual. Men often have a great need for the cleansing of their imaginations; they often struggle with temptations toward masturbation and an intense fantasy life. Mario Bergner contends that men keep the pornography business thriving.

When I first confessed my struggle with sexual fantasy during my college years, I expected my friend and confessor to recoil in horror. Instead I found that he struggled with the same problem, and so did many other guys he knew well.

Women are told in Genesis 3 that their desire will be for their husband. This desire is not the God-given desire that characterized their initial creation, but the frustrated desire that characterizes our relationships today. Women tend to find their identity in a relationship with a man. They can feel they are not a person if they are not in such a relationship. Their bentness is often toward men and the approval and attention of men.

Female idolatry is often emotional and relational. Their temptation is to build relationships of emotional dependency and enmeshment. They also face the temptation to give themselves away physically in order to get what they need emotionally. Women, according to Bergner, keep the romantic fantasy business thriving.

With the loss of mothering in our day and the tendency of unaffirmed men to hurt or abuse their daughters, women can also turn away from men entirely, seeking affirmation and practicing emotional dependency solely with other women.

So how do we help people experience transformation in their sexual and gender identity?

First, we must teach the biblical truths of our God-created, God-redeemed identity as men and women in Christ. People need to know that they are a new creation, that the old self has died with Christ, that they have been raised to new life, and that by the Spirit they are given the power to live in accordance with what they already are.

Second, we must teach them a process that helps them regularly appropriate the power of God to live in their true identity in Christ. That process includes

1. living out of the power and reality of their union with Christ
2. renouncing and forsaking their idolatry and false identities
3. receiving and extending forgiveness
4. aligning their will with God's will and receiving strengthening for their will
5. looking to God for healing and filling
6. choosing to meet their genuine needs in God-given ways
7. learning to minister to others in ways that heal and fill and encourage transformation

The teaching from Genesis and the prayers that follow both illustrate the process and are a resource for ministry that you can take and begin to use immediately among your postmodern friends who come to know Jesus.

First we practice God's presence and tune our ears and our hearts to his voice. Jesus put it this way:

Before long, the world will not see me anymore, but you will see me. Because I live, you also will live. On that day you will realize that I am in my Father, and you are in me, and I am in you. If anyone loves me, he will obey my teaching. My Father will love him, and we will come to him and make our home with him. (Jn 14:19-23)

Pray and affirm these truths. Another lives in you. Hallelujah! The God of the universe, the Creator of planets and stars, the Redeemer who died for you and now lives and reigns is one with you by the Spirit. How can you *not* experience healing and transformation?

Next, we must repent of our false identities. We must renounce these forms of idolatry. They will have spiritual power over us until we do. But we do not repent of the created human needs we have. We repent of the inhuman and self-centered ways we have sought to meet those needs. And we seek the strengthening of our will, which has been weakened by the practice of idolatry and dependency.

Some of us need emotional divorces from past and present dependent and sexually expressive relationships.

Before offering prayers that help in this process, I need to say a word about the imagination. In our Western modern approach to discipleship, we have often been good at bringing our rational thoughts under the lordship of Christ. But we have often let the devil have our imaginations. The imagination and the symbols and pictures we carry in our hearts are often more powerful in determining our identity and behavior than our rational thoughts. The imagination and its symbols and images are the bridge between the head and the heart. Unless our imagination comes under the lordship of Christ, our identity will be left divided, with our head telling us one thing about who we are and our heart and imagination telling us something very different.

We need to *resymbolize* our views of God, others, ourselves and the world around us to come into alignment with truth. We need new symbols of heaven. We need to recover a truly biblical imagination. We need new symbols of the human person. Our current symbols are so material, so one-dimensional, so nontranscendent. We often teach rationally about the glory of men and women, made in the image of God, yet we carry inner pictures and symbols of men and women that are tawdry, dark and rooted in lust more than love. Thus the prayers that follow help to integrate our imaginative grasp of truth with our rational understanding of truth. Only in this way will we experience transformation that has depth and power in all of who we are, in our rational and our imaginative dimensions.

So back to the process of leading others into transformation. The following prayers capture the steps we can lead others through. These prayers, especially those for the strengthening of the will, are adapted from *The Healing Presence* (Payne, p. 64).

> *I pray, Lord, for the release and strengthening of my will, that with which I initiate change and choose life, and with which I forsake the bent, idolatrous position of attempting to find my identity in other people or other things.*

> *Show me any way in which I am bent toward the creature; O Lord, reveal any idolatrous dependency on persons or things. Show me any way I demand from the created the identity I can gain only from you, my Creator.*

Visualize (see with your heart) any bentness the Lord is showing you; then see yourself deliberately straightening up from that idol as you pray:

> *I choose, Lord, to forsake this bentness, I confess it to you, just now, as the sin, the idol, that it is. I renounce it in your name. And I thank you for your forgiveness. I receive your forgiveness and cleansing.*

To one another you can now proclaim forgiveness. "To those who truly repent, I proclaim you forgiven, in Christ's name. Receive this forgiveness now into your heart." Then pray:

> *Come into me, divine, initiating, eternal Will. Lord, command what you will, and then will what you command.*

> *I thank you, Lord, that my weak and insufficient will is now one with yours. May I know more and more what it means to be in-willed, indwelt by you. Thank you, Lord, that your completing, healing work is commenced in me and will continue in this world and the next.*

Write in your prayer journal the images of bentness you saw toward mother or father, husband or wife, son or daughter, someone of the same sex or other sex, any way you have made an idol of job, money, fame or self: then converse with God about them. He will give you understanding of them and enable you to begin to get at the roots of the idolatries or dependencies that have held you back from full freedom in him.

Now visualize the cross between you and the person or thing you were bent toward. See Jesus coming between you and that person, setting a holy boundary, protecting you from hurtful or dependency-building acts and words. Now see yourself giving the pieces of their heart back to this person, pieces of their heart that weren't theirs to give you. See yourself taking back the pieces of your heart that weren't yours to give this person. You can tell that person what you are doing and why, and you can ask their forgiveness, and extend yours, for the emotional or physical union that was not healthy or appropriate to the relationship.

Now celebrate! Give thanks to God for his mighty presence with you and within you.

> *God, fill me now with your light and your love. Replace the empty places that were filled with distorted images and dependent relationships. Fill me with your presence, with your light, with images of the good and the true and the beautiful. Spirit of God, now fill me from the bottom of my toes to the top of my head; fill every cell of my being with your presence. Come, Holy Spirit. Fill me and use me, I pray. For I give you all thanks and all glory and all praise.*
>
> *I choose now to meet my God-given needs in God-glorifying and health-giving ways. And I ask, Lord, that you will teach me to minister to others in the way you are now ministering to me. For I pray in your name. Amen.*

These prayers can be prayed alone, one on one or with a group. Only after God has led your own soul through the process can you lead others. It would be a mistake to too quickly start leading others using these prayers. We must learn the skill of listening to God, and we also must have experienced some real transformation in these areas of our lives if we are to have the wisdom to lead others well.

It is also important to remember that this process involves the work of God's Spirit and is carried on primarily in community. In many of our Christian traditions we have lost sight of the importance of confessing our sins to one another, of receiving the announcement of forgiveness from one another. James 5:16 is clear: our experience of forgiveness, healing and transformation is tied to our confession to and prayer for one another. Sin makes us sick physically, emotionally and spiritually. God uses our confessions of sin to one another and our prayers for one another to make us each more whole!

We can be channels of God's healing and transformation to one another, through confession, through prayer, through laying on of hands and through the appropriate meeting of genuine human needs.

The sacraments can be of great help to us also. The sacraments can become channels of God's grace and transformation. God uses matter. He *likes* it. After all, he made it. And in Christ God filled flesh and took it into his very being.

Learning to walk daily in our true identity in Christ is a long obedience in the same direction. Often we face a besetting idolatry, a besetting sin. This area of greatest struggle is likely related to deep rejection or hurt. At those places of hurt, the temptation toward idolatry is great. We need continually to recognize our bentness, to renounce it, to worship God and practice his presence, to commit ourselves to relationships of love, encouragement and accountability with others who know us and our darker side. As we do, we will experience the progressive transformation that we long for, that will be winsome and contagious to others in our postmodern, identity-hungry world. We will have an ever new, ever fresh story of transformation to tell. We will have good news! Glory to God!

Stories of transformed lives are the greatest apologetic we have in a postmodern world. God is transforming lives by healing people at deep levels of being in our day. And for that we give God thanks and praise.

Discussion Questions

1. In what areas have you experienced real change since coming to Christ? What has most helped you to experience change in your life?

2. Do you agree that the church has often not provided much help in the areas of woundedness and sin that keep plaguing us? Do you agree that we need much more help from God and others in areas of sexuality, gender identity and relationships? Why or why not?

3. Look at Ephesians 4:17—5:20. What do you learn here about the new self and the old self and how to nurture one and starve the other? What are some of the idolatries people were bent toward in Paul's day, and where do you see those same idolatries in contemporary life?

4. In what ongoing struggle do you need to experience more of God's transformational help and power? What do you tend to be bent toward or have too central in your life?

5. What perspectives and prayers were or could be most helpful to you from that section of this chapter (pp. 148-49)?

6. Do you have a mentor who could help you pray and work through these prayers? Could you start a journal to help you work through some of these issues in an ongoing way?

15

GETTING & STAYING OUTSIDE THE BOX

GOD IS PROFOUNDLY AT WORK IN OUR DAY TO REACH EXPERIENTIAL, COMMUNITY-seeking postmodern people. We have been looking at what God is doing and what strategies and models God seems to be blessing to reach people today. But what's your part to play, and how can you discern that part? None of us can do all the things that are in this book—and in all the other good books on evangelism! None of us has all the gifts or all the resources. So how do we choose what to do and what not to do? Where do we start?

We start with our heart. The story of Pam can help us. Pam was an experiential, community-seeking postmodern student at the University of Wisconsin-Madison. In her first year, she was excited about new freedoms but felt as if something important was missing from her life. I'll let her tell the rest.

> My friend Sue invited me to a Christian meeting one Friday night, and not
> wanting to offend her, I went along. The meeting was dismal—a boring skit
> and some weak singing. Sue was mortified. And then this gangly-looking fel-

low with broken glasses [the author!] stood up on a chair and announced there would be a prayer meeting afterwards and anyone who wanted to stay was invited to do so.

Apologizing for the dismal meeting, my friend Sue asked if I was ready to go, but the Holy Spirit was arousing my curiosity and I told her I'd stay. The prayer time began. It was the most awesome and wonderful prayer meeting I have ever attended. In that short hour, my eyes and soul were opened to the King of kings and Lord of lords. To this day, I remember snippets of things prayed for during that time. I realized right then and there that I wanted that kind of relationship with God. About one month later, Rick sat me down and shared the gospel directly and I trusted Christ. It was the most precious moment of my life.

Later Pam was proposed to while baby-sitting my kids! She went on to become an urban missionary in Philadelphia.

Don't you want to see your friends and family have their eyes opened to the King of kings and Lord of lords? Don't you want them to be with you in heaven forever? Won't you miss them and grieve if they're not?

Prayer and Multiplication
You can see miracles like Pam's happen with your experiential, community-seeking postmodern friends. Start praying, for your friends and with your friends. Cry out to God. Start with your heart.

Then take a next step. Invite your friends to a group investigating God (GIG) that you will lead. If you are new to this, recruit someone else to lead it with you. Or begin with a genuine, seeker-friendly prayer time. If your fellowship or church can launch soul-awakening events *and* some next step in community for seekers at the same time, that's even better. But a few simple steps taken over time by a couple of passionate, praying people can turn your church or ministry upside down.

My friend Becky invited her friends to a GIG. She explained her desire to her Christian fellowship group and got them praying for her. One week she asked one of her pre-Christian friends to tell the fellowship group how it was going. The friend explained to the group that she wasn't a Christian but was enjoying looking at Jesus. She told a couple of funny stories about Becky's mistakes. Members of the fellowship group loved that part!

Several weeks later the friend committed her life to Christ. Becky asked her to come back and share her story with the whole fellowship. She did, and at the end the group erupted in applause. Becky then asked if others would want to lead a GIG. Twenty people responded and came to a training time Becky led. Soon Becky was helping fellowship groups all over the Midwest start GIGs.

Transformational miracles like this start with a few simple steps you could take today. Get your church or ministry praying for you every step of the way. If someone gives their life to Christ, have them tell their story to everyone in your church or ministry. The electric adventure of reaching those outside God's family will have begun—for you and for everyone who is praying for you.

Becoming God's Partner

God is raising up a movement of evangelism through local churches and ministries in our day. The seeker church movement (from Willow Creek Community Church) and the purpose-driven church movement (from Saddleback Church) are only two of a multitude of great examples. So are the rapid spread of the Alpha course, the multiplication of GIGs, and the exploding connection between worship and evangelism. God is at work to reach postmodern people.

God is pouring out his Spirit to heal the sick and find the lost. Postmodern people are helped toward the kingdom by authentic Spirit-filled community and by genuine God experiences. It is no accident that many renewal movements exploded into our culture in the 1960s, when the postmodern mindset also exploded into our culture. God is indeed at work to reach experience-oriented, community-seeking postmodern people.

Campus ministries are growing. New churches for the next generation are being planted. Denominations and Christians are pouring resources and time into an unprecedented wave of planting new churches around the world. God is at work to reach all people, and maybe especially postmodern people.

Do you want to be part of what God is doing?

Let God challenge your theological, sacred practice, structure, strategy and self-perception boxes.

Ask God to tune your ears and hearts to the new questions people are asking, and the new ways to respond that will be attractive, relevant and true to life for them.

Pursue a simple strategy that will serve the process the pre-Christians around you need. Work in and through *teams*. Build *friendships* with pre-Christians, and *pray* for and with them. Hold *soul-awakening events* monthly, or as often as you can with excellence. Launch Alpha or GIGs to draw pre-Christians into seeking *community*. Challenge them to *conversion*, using *Circles of Belonging* or some other gospel presentation. Invite them into *transformation* through healing prayer and small group community.

Ask God for the courage and wisdom to help you and others lead your church or ministry into evangelism outside the box!

May God bless the work of his Spirit in and through us to reap a great and mighty harvest in an increasingly postmodern world. May many experiential and community-seeking postmodern people come home to God in our day.

Amen! And to God be the glory.

Discussion Questions

As you think back over the book you have just finished, what do you remember most vividly? What have you learned? How have you been encouraged? What are your next steps? Spend some time in prayer. And then go talk with a person who is still outside God's family.

God will bless you and be with you as you go. That's his promise.

Afterword: To Pastors and Leaders of Churches & Ministries

How do we lead people into changes needed to reach those outside God's family? How do we lead a church or ministry into evangelism outside the box?

This afterword is addressed to those who have responsibility to lead others in reaching those outside God's family. It gives you some steps to take in helping your whole church or ministry become passionate and fruitful in witness.

Prior Questions

Before you initiate change, it is important to honestly face your strengths and liabilities as a church or ministry. Are you starting from scratch, planting a church or fellowship group? You are fortunate! You can set reaching those outside God's family as a core priority and then design your ministry and implement the priorities and suggestions of this book in a full-orbed way. You will probably lack resources, but you will not be fighting tradition. Value your beginning, however hard and challenging: it provides a wonderful opportunity.

Are you an established ministry with a long and strong tradition? You will have resources and leaders, but the effort to bring change will be demanding and difficult. You will need wisdom and a careful Spirit-filled process for healthy change. Even young churches can be set in their ways. The larger you are, the more resources you have, but the harder it will be to bring change. The older your ministry is, the more you will have to search your collective soul, and the greater will be the spiritual battle as you seek to increase your fruitfulness in witness.

Your honest assessment can help you decide whether to launch radical change or whether to start small. Either way, you will need to declare war, to give your best energy and efforts to see real and lasting change in reaching the lost.

You will also need to discern your calling to reach ethnically and culturally diverse people. If you are called to reach out across ethnic and cultural barriers, you will need some diversity in your leadership team. Leaders of another ethnicity or culture will help you understand their group's felt needs and the culturally sensitive ways to meet those needs.

So then, what is needed to bring transformational change in your church or ministry? How can your ministry take a quantum leap forward in its priority, passion and potency in reaching those outside God's family?

Steps Toward Transformation

Start with prayer! Cry out to God for your friends. Begin to ask at every board, committee, small group and prayer meeting how things are with members' pre-Christian friends. Join with and lead people in corporate prayer about reaching those around you. You can begin prayer times like those of the Madison freshmen (see chapter ten). Prayer meetings that are worshipful, simple, honest about sin and fervent about the lost can be used by God to change the world. As you pray, God will bless you and help you and your people reach your friends. They are more on his heart than they are on yours.

Read Jim Cymbala's fine book *Fresh Wind, Fresh Fire*, about the way God used prayer (and gospel music) to turn a church upside down.

Then lead a process that will help your ministry get focused on reaching those outside the family. Mark Mittelberg offers these insights:

1. *Take a step yourself to build a friendship and reach a friend.* You can only motivate people to go where you are already going. Otherwise you will merely increase everyone's guilt feelings.

If you are focusing on the needs of a pre-Christian friend, every new step you plan for your church or ministry will be designed with your friend in mind. That will help you and your church more than you can know!

2. *Begin to communicate your vision and passion for evangelism.* Vision for evangelism leaks away. Often it even gushes away. Come back to your

vision and heart month by month, and use every means you can to get people on board. Teach from the Scriptures and share personal stories. Express your hunger and hope to see a stream of freshly redeemed people entering and energizing your ministry. When people see your heart is genuine, they will respond with enthusiasm.

A key here is to *establish a sense of urgency for reaching people today*. People need to see your heart, feel God's heart and realize that many of us are just not seeing much fruitfulness. We are in an urgent crisis, a crisis that involves our priorities, our heart, our faithfulness and our fruitfulness. Until we see and feel the crisis, we won't have much energy for change and sacrifice.

Deepen your passion and urgency by calling people to pray and by taking leaders to observe ministries that are bearing fruit. Seeing other fruitful ministries helps shatter our complacency and increase our faith.

3. *Look for someone to partner with in leading your church or ministry in evangelism.* The senior leader needs to set the priority and value of evangelism and needs to model relational evangelism in some way. But the senior leader can't do it all. If you are a senior leader, you need a point person for evangelism in your church or ministry. That person should have a passion for reaching the lost and some relational and leadership skills at building a team.

Ultimately this person needs to be on staff with you. But you can start with a gifted and committed volunteer. The two of you can then become partners in leading your church or ministry into reaching people outside God's family. As the focus is established, the point person then leads out in the remaining steps.

4. *Train your people in relational evangelism.* The best curriculum I know is the Becoming a Contagious Christian course, and the university edition of that course is great for training postmodern people. Get the curriculum from Zondervan Publishing House (616-698-0802), and get the university edition video from InterVarsity Christian Fellowship (608-274-9001).

5. *Invite interested and passionate people who have taken the course onto an evangelism team.* Let them tell their stories and exhort one another to faith and action. The embers of our evangelistic fire gradually die out if we stand alone. But when we gather as people who share a heart for the lost, those embers can build into a blazing bonfire. As we share our stories and our passion, we once again become contagious Christians and build a conta-

gious church or ministry.

6. *The evangelism team can develop appropriate outreach programs and efforts.* The team may put together soul-awakening events or launch GIGs or the Alpha course.

As you launch events and efforts, *seek and celebrate short-term gains.* Here is where many efforts at growing in evangelism falter. If we go too long without any fruit or celebration, we will gradually lose interest and urgency to reach the lost. Then people will get tired of any new attempts to motivate them. So make sure to implement outreach that has a good shot at reaching people in the near future, and then celebrate every interim victory, every Christian who gets in the game of reaching people, every person who takes a step toward Christ or comes to Christ. Have new Christians share their story with your whole church or ministry. Celebrate baptisms, whether they are many or few, with exuberant joy!

The Alpha program often yields these short-term wins. So do GIGs. Sometimes it takes a couple of years to learn how to put together soul-awakening events well. In the meantime, make sure your people are involved in direct relational evangelism efforts at sharing their faith. And celebrate!

As you begin to see an increase in passion and participation in witness, redouble your efforts. Don't slow down or rest on a few initial victories. Commit to the long haul. It takes time for vision and passion for evangelism to really become a part of your heart and ministry culture. And trying to reverse flagging momentum is like trying to stop a boulder rolling downhill.

So as you begin to see change, invite *more* people into the process. Invite your worship leader, your kids' ministry leader, your social events leader, your teaching pastors and other key leaders to think and work together so that every part of your ministry reflects a passionate concern for pre-Christian people. As every leader begins to sing the same song and work together on reaching people, your ministry and your people will be transformed—and everything you do as a church or ministry will be filled with excitement and energy.

The Steps: A Short List
In summary, how do you lead your church or ministry into greater evangelistic passion and effectiveness? Begin with prayer, with crying out to God,

and with asking people at every gathering how it is going with their friends. Then lead a process of growth and change that includes the following steps developed by Mittelberg:

Step 1. *Own and model* the value of personal relational evangelism.

Step 2. *Communicate* your vision and heart for reaching those outside God's family. Build urgency and passion.

Step 3. *Name a point person* to lead further evangelism efforts.

Step 4. *Train* everyone in relational evangelism.

Step 5. Recruit an evangelism *team*.

Step 6. With the team, develop *soul-awakening events* and *community experiences* for pre-Christians. As you see progress, invite more and more of your leaders to partner in the process of inviting people to come home to God.

The senior leader leads out in the first three steps, and the evangelism point person leads in the next three steps, with the senior leader's help and support.

A multitude of ideas, resources and examples can be found in Mittelberg's book *Building a Contagious Church*. It's full of stories of ways churches and ministries are living out these steps. John Kotter's outstanding book *Leading Change* can also help, especially if your ministry is large or has some traditions that are seeker unfriendly. Kotter's delineation of the change process is profoundly insightful and challenging.

The Question of Influence
You may have the influence to lead a process like this. Start by communicating the need and bringing some people together to discuss this chapter and this book.

But you may not believe you have the influence to help lead a process like this. What should you do? Give this book (or chapter) to your senior leader and anyone else who leads outreach efforts in your church or ministry. They need to be on board and provide overall leadership. But as you pray, reach out and offer your time and energy to those leaders, God may use *you* to help lead your church or group into a new day in witness. Wouldn't it be glorious if God renewed your church or group in reaching people so that many of your friends and family members came home to God? It would transform you, your ministry, and your pre-Christian friends—for eternity.

Discussion Questions

1. Evaluate your ministry's strengths and liabilities in evangelism. Are you ready to launch radical change, or should you start small?

2. Look over the process for increasing your evangelistic passion and effectiveness. Would this process help you and your ministry? What are some steps you could take? Whom could you invite to join you in reading this book and thinking about how your ministry can grow in reaching people?

3. What role could the senior leader play in helping your ministry grow in witness? Who could play the role of point person for evangelism?

4. If you are reading and discussing this book with others, spend some time coming up with a plan for leading your people and your ministry into growing evangelistic passion and fruitfulness. Use the steps listed above as the outline for your plan.

5. Pray! Cry out to God, the Lord of the harvest and the lover of souls. Pray for a time of great harvest in *this* generation!

Appendix 1

THE RISE & FALL
OF THE MODERN WORLD

WHAT DO WE NEED TO UNDERSTAND ABOUT THE POSTMODERN MIND IN ORDER to communicate the gospel effectively to the next generation? Above all, we need to grasp the nature and immensity of the epochal change in mindset.

The Rise of the Modern World
One of my favorite reads growing up was Isaac Asimov's Foundation trilogy. Asimov tells the story of the fall of a Galactic Empire centuries in the future. The story also involves the rise of a new world order based on a new science of the mind.

The trilogy opens up with a trial of Hari Seldon, the man who has founded the new science of the mind that will raise up a new world from the ashes of the old. Seldon, using what he calls the mathematics of psychohistory, which predicts the behavior of large masses of people, has predicted the fall of the Galactic Empire. He is on trial for treason.

> Seldon: The fall of the Empire, gentlemen, is a massive thing, however, and not easily fought. It is dictated by a rising bureaucracy, a receding initiative, a freezing of caste, a damming of curiosity—a hundred other factors. It has been going on, as I have said, for centuries, and it is too majestic and massive to stop.

Prosecutor: Is it not obvious to anyone that the Empire is as strong as it ever was?

Seldon: The appearance of strength is all about you. It would seem to last forever. However, Mr. [Prosecutor], the rotten tree-trunk, until the very moment when the storm-blast breaks it in two, has all the appearance of might it ever had. Listen with the ears of psychohistory, and you will hear the creaking. (Asimov, p. 29)

The appearance of strength, our technological and military wonders, is all about us. It would seem to last forever. But the worldview and ethical values that gave rise to this strength are crumbling. Even now you can hear the winds of a coming storm blast that will show the weakness at the heart of our way of life. How have we come to this point? What are the signs of our weakness?

The modern world rose like the dawn out of the dark and corrupt days of the late medieval Roman Church. Now the signs are everywhere that the cultural vision that rose with Isaac Newton and René Descartes is now crumbling, turning back in upon itself. The final decade in which the modern worldview had pervasive cultural influence was the 1960s, the decade of the moon landing, the Peace Corps, the dream of Martin Luther King Jr., the Camelot of President John Kennedy, the Great Society of President Lyndon Johnson, the TV show *Star Trek* (my favorite). Yet this was also the decade of Vietnam, the assassinations of John and Bobby Kennedy, of Martin Luther King Jr., the final decade of heroes before Watergate in 1972. In the bloody and riotous 1960s, dreams and heroes died, as author Arthur Levine put it. So did the modern cultural vision.

The sixties started with King's dream of a more just society based on the content of our character and the guiding beacon of freedom. The sixties ended with black power, a politics justifying violence in response to violence, and an ethic based on the needs and consciousness of the group. This shift from King's vision for universal human progress to Malcolm X's vision for black identity, black history and black power is paradigmatic of the larger shift from a modern to a postmodern world. In the late 1960s and early 1970s a postmodern vision and philosophy began to infiltrate academia; by now it has largely swept our culture. But how is the death of a pervasive worldview coming about?

To understand, we must return to the founders of the modern cultural vision: Nicolaus Copernicus (1473-1543), Galileo Galilei (1564-1642), Isaac

Newton (1642-1727), René Descartes (1596-1650) and Francis Bacon (1561-1626). Two great intellectual mysteries have engaged the rational mind since its rise in the classical Greek culture of old: the mystery of the movement of the planets and the stars in the heavens, and the mystery of human consciousness. Copernicus began the revolution in the way Western culture viewed the mystery of movement in the heavens by positing a heliocentric (sun) centered universe. Up to that time, the earth had been considered the center of the universe, and humans were considered the crown of creation. Galileo, with his telescope, proved the hypothesis of a sun-centered solar system, and Johannes Kepler (1571-1630) developed the theory of the elliptical orbit of the planets. Newton, born on Christmas the year Galileo died, established the fundamental laws of motion and gravity.

The Creator became a divine architect, a master mathematician and clock-maker, while the universe was now viewed as a uniformly regulated and fundamentally impersonal phenomenon running on its own perfect, immutable, mathematical laws. People had penetrated the universe's essential order and could now use that knowledge for their own benefit and empowerment.

Francis Bacon in England helped develop one great principle of knowledge that drove the Enlightenment: empiricism expressed in the inductive method. Philosopher John Locke (1632-1704) later put it this way: "There is nothing in the intellect not previously in the senses" (quoted in Tarnas, p.333). The first foundation of knowledge is the senses. The key activity of the knower is observation and collection of data through the senses.

Descartes developed the other great principle of knowledge that drove the Enlightenment: rationalism. Through the process of inner reflection on empirical data, the mind could discover and know the truth about the world. Descartes began by doubting everything. He ended with the conclusion that the only thing he couldn't doubt was that there was a self that was doubting. *Cogito ergo sum.* "I think, therefore I am." He could have said, "I doubt, therefore I am." Descartes then sought to build all the rest of knowledge, including knowledge about God, on this foundation of reason.

Four key inventions helped make this scientific approach and its results known throughout the world (Tarnas, p. 225). The magnetic compass permitted navigational feats. Gunpowder contributed to the demise of the feudal system and the rise of the nation-state. The mechanical clock liberated human beings from the rule of the seasons. The printing press brought an explosion of learning and a spread of innovation and new thought across the known world.

The expansion of the scientific revolution and the Reformation would have been impossible without the printing press.

The new approach to knowing, when coupled with key inventions, drove the scientific revolution, but even more gave birth to a powerful new cultural vision that has guided the West through four centuries of achievement and technological progress. The final dénouement of the medieval Judeo-Christian worldview came at the halfway point, with the theory of evolution and the application of Charles Darwin's (1809-1882) work to a culminating modern vision of a world that was understandable without God. With Copernicus, the world was no longer at the center of the universe. With Darwin, humans were no longer the crown of creation. Rather, they were the product of an eons-long process of random variation and natural selection, surviving only because of the accidental development of consciousness. Consciousness made humans the most fit of the animals to survive. Consciousness was merely an accident, a byproduct of time and chance and struggle. What a long way people had fallen from their perch at the top of the created order, made in the image of God, inhabiting a paradise of harmony and fruitfulness!

Yet for moderns, what a long way humans had come. Humanity had come of age, throwing off psychological dependency on an omnipotent Parent in the sky, emerging from the womb of the world to control human destiny and exploit and rule nature.

Proclaiming the Gospel in a Modern World

Proclamation of the gospel within the modern worldview was born in the Reformation. Such proclamation was an appeal to the individual's mind and will, the individual who stands autonomous before God and whose choice determines his destiny. The proclamation of the gospel was fleshed out by profound intellectual attempts at proving the existence of God and by an apologetics of the mind focusing on the challenges of modernity to Christian faith. Attacks on miracles by philosopher David Hume (1711-1776) and others were met with a vigorous defense of the faith, marshaling historical and logical proofs that would be compelling for the modern, rational, empirical mind.

Christianity was expected to disintegrate under the modernist onslaught and be laid to rest without much ado as the superstitious and oppressive system it was, appropriate for a more archaic and ignorant age, but no longer needed for humanity come of age. But Christian faith did not shrivel up and die. Rather it met the modernist challenge creatively and vigorously and has grown to claim the allegiance of over 1.5 billion people around the world in our day. This relative success ought to give us hope that as the ground under us changes from modern to postmodern, the church can rise up again, reformulate what we communicate, and grow and flourish in a new era of human history.

The Fall of the Modern Mind

The real casualty of the modern enterprise has not been Christianity but the modern mind itself. How did the compelling and powerful cultural vision that has produced so many technological wonders come to lose its potency?

The modern vision carried within it the seeds of is own dissolution. The twin principles of rationalism and empiricism, when applied consistently to life, including the life of the mind, have resulted in the loss of the good of reason. The story of the self-destruction of the modern mind is a long one, beginning soon after the ascendancy of the modern worldview. Certain key points in the story help us understand the genesis and nature of the postmodern mind.

One key moment is the development of the remarkable philosophy of Immanuel Kant (1724-1804). Copernicus had explained the apparent movement of the heavens by postulating the real movement of the observer and the earth on which the observer stood. Kant explained the apparent order of the observable world by locating that order *in the mind of the observer.* We cannot know anything for what it really is. We can know only what our mind reports that it is. We know the world our senses report to us only through the interpretive grid of the structures of our mind. And we can't know anything at all about the world of the spiritual and invisible, for there we don't even have any sensory impressions to go on.

Kant didn't intend to take away all basis for objective knowledge, but in the end that is what he did. After Kant, in the modern mind there is only subjective knowledge, knowledge that has been profoundly influenced by the subject before it can be known.

Another key moment in the gradual loss of the reliability of reason was the psychology of Sigmund Freud (1856-1939), who was followed by others like Carl Jung (1875-1961). Freud, using empirical and rational principles in his study of human consciousness, uncovered the unconscious mind. "Underneath man's rationality was a cauldron of unconscious biological instincts—amoral, aggressive, erotic, and 'polymorphous perverse.' Rationality, moral conscience, and religious feelings were conceivably no more than reaction-formations and delusions of the civilized self-concept" (Tarnas, p. 328).

If Freud revealed a personal unconscious world, Karl Marx (1818-1883) revealed a social unconscious mind (Tarnas, p. 329). Marx postulated that the philosophical, religious and moral values of each age were inextricably tied to the most powerful class's attempt to control the means of production. Human cultural values, psychological motivations and conscious awareness were historically relative phenomena derived from unconscious political, economic and instinctual impulses of an entirely naturalistic quality.

These thinkers demonstrated the irony of the modern mind. As Tarnas puts it, the more modern persons strove to control nature by understanding its principles, to free themselves from nature's power, to separate themselves from nature's necessity and rise above it, the more completely their science metaphysically submerged humanity into nature, and thus into its mechanistic and impersonal character (Tarnas, p. 332).

In the twentieth century scientists joined the philosophers, psychologists and sociologists in the growing overthrow of the mechanized, mathematical, manipulable world of the modern mind.

Another major blow to the modern vision came at the dawn of the 1960s, when Thomas Kuhn (1922-1996) developed a whole new theory for how science advances. In his overview of scientific progress Kuhn saw that prevailing paradigms are self-validating, conflicting data are explained away, and progress is made by radical shifts of vision in which a multitude of rational and nonrational factors play a part.

Twentieth-century history undid common illusions of the inevitability of progress. Two world wars, the Holocaust, nuclear technology that could destroy the world at the push of a button, ethnic wars and ethnic cleansing, the environmental affects of technology, and the war between the sexes have eradicated the optimistic hope that the modernist cultural project would lead to a utopia of harmony, progress and well-being for all.

Philosopher G. W. F. Hegel (1770-1831), the last visionary for a comprehensive, evolutionary world order based on the modernist impulse, finally undid even the fundamental tenet of logic that had shaped Western thought since Aristotle, the law of noncontradiction. For Hegel, history travels an evolutionary path in which every event (thesis) inevitably leads to its opposite (antithesis). The two combine (synthesis) to create a new, more advanced reality and consciousness. Logic is synthetic. Opposites do attract, combining to drive history upward into new and better evolutionary states. To thinkers since Hegel, our attempts at defending the faith based solely on the law of noncontradiction seem simplistic and dichotomizing.

As we entered the 1970s, reason was no longer certain but was rather the function of a myriad of factors, instinctual and unknown. Society was the story of the powerful oppressing the poor to keep power. Technology was an instrument in the hands of the powerful to maintain power and to rape the environment for personal gain. Science had unlocked the secrets of the universe and found a relative, elusive, irrational and uncertain order to the world. God was dead, and so was virtue. As the modernist person grasped history with his intellect, reality went to pieces in his hands and fragmented, meaning disintegrated, and reason lost its center.

Postmoderns have finished the process of undercutting the modern cultural mind. The most articulate and characteristic postmoderns have been the scholars of language. They tell us that all human thought is bound by cultural-linguistic forms. Language is a "cage" (Wittgenstein). Language is a construct with no necessary connection to an objective reality. Texts are always full of tensions and contradictions. Meaning can never be fixed and determined. We understand texts only by entering into them and standing under them. We change a text's meaning whenever we enter a text. In the end, there is no secure basis of truth or meaning outside the "cage."

Postmodernism is the final unmasking and unmaking of the modern mind.

> On its own terms, the assertion of the historical relativity and cultural-linguistic bondage of all truth and knowledge must itself be regarded as reflecting one more local and temporal perspective having no necessarily universal, extra-historical value. Everything could change tomorrow. Implicitly, the one postmodern absolute is critical consciousness, which by deconstructing all, seems compelled by its own logic to do so to itself as well. This is the unstable paradox that permeates the postmodern mind. (Tarnas, p. 402)

Will the disintegration of the modern mind continue, spinning out ever new and more diverse and fragmented ideas and conceptions of the world? Or are these the days of the final loss of faith in the world that will precede the radical end-times intervention of God in the return of Christ? Or is the stage set for a new reintegration of the world mind, the birth of a new cultural vision that will guide the history of the West, and maybe the history of the world, over the next several centuries? What will this new cultural vision be called, if it emerges?

We are a culture in transition. Just as it took time for the modern worldview to dominate, it will take time for whatever comes next to gain dominance. Many medievalists carried on into the Modern era. There will be many moderns who carry on into the postmodern era. The focus of this book is on anticipating and adapting to the change that is coming. However, there are many people today for whom a modern approach to proclaiming the gospel will still be compelling. In that sense, reports of the demise of modernism are premature and exaggerated.

Appendix 2

LEADING A GIG

A GROUP INVESTIGATING GOD (GIG) IS FOR PEOPLE WHO ARE ON A SPIRITUAL search. They are looking for love, belonging and meaning. And they are willing to look at and discuss what Jesus might have to teach us. These groups are also called investigative Bible discussions or seeker small groups, and you may have another great name!

A GIG looks at the biographies of Jesus. The group discovers together what Jesus does and says and what wisdom he has to give.

GIGs are helpful and powerful because they create a place of dialogue and discovery to look at issues that are important in all our lives. We let the Scriptures speak to people directly. And we let people see how attractive, relevant and real Jesus is. People today are looking for attractiveness, relevance and reality, when it comes to whom they will follow and learn from. Jesus uniquely embodies all those qualities.

GIGs need to be safe places for people to ask questions and express ideas, especially if they are not yet committed Christians. Therefore the committed Christians need to be a silent minority. It is amazing to see how God uses those outside the family of God to influence each other, especially when they can ask their questions honestly and without fear of being corrected or preached at. Thus the number of Christians in the group always needs to be equal to (if the group is one on one or two on two) or less than the number of those outside the family.

GIGs can be one on one or larger. They work well either way. People today are longing for experiences of community and connection to one another; GIGs encourage strong relationships and honest sharing of our struggles.

GIGs can run for a half-hour to an hour, but not longer. To start, people need to be able to commit themselves to only a short time. These groups meet for four to six weeks at most, and then people can decide if they want to keep going.

GIGs are a fabulous way for Christians to share their relationship with God, and they are a fabulous way for those outside the family to find God. Almost anyone can lead a GIG, and almost everyone will benefit by being part of one.

How Do I Get Started?

1. Pray for friends and family who are outside God's family, and ask God to show you people you can ask to be part of a GIG.

2. Start and strengthen your friendships with people outside God's family. Just spend time with them. Look for opportunities to care for them. Do something fun, or have a meal with them. Include them in your regular activities.

3. Ask God to give you courage, boldness and discernment for when you should ask people to be part of your GIG and for whom you should ask.

4. Invite people to join you in a GIG. This step is the biggest hump to get over. But if you can get up the guts to ask, and if God gives wisdom as you ask, people will often say yes. Even people you didn't expect will say yes. But they can't say yes until you ask them! More help on the invitation will be given below.

5. Pick a time and place to meet. I often meet people in their home or place of work or dorm room, because then they are sure to be there! If the meeting is in your home or room, you can offer to swing by and pick up your guests as a helpful reminder.

6. Create a warm environment, welcome them in a heartfelt way, and provide refreshments.

7. Start the discussion. It will help greatly if you give a few guidelines (suggested below). Then make sure everyone, and especially any Christian in the group, follows the guidelines.

8. Have an excellent discussion (suggested studies and helps below).

9. Invite people back next week.

10. Develop the friendship during the week, whether they come back or

not. Don't feel pressure to discuss spiritual concepts. Keep the friendship on a fun and normal level.

How Do I Invite People?
1. Pray for them.
2. Figure out exactly what you want to say in your invitation. Write it out beforehand.
3. Say something like this: "I've enjoyed our discussions about spiritual issues. I am beginning a group for people who are not necessarily sure of what they believe but are willing to discuss spiritual issues with others. We will look at the biographies of Jesus and get wisdom from him and from each other. We'll meet for four weeks, for only forty-five minutes a time. We'll focus on issues of relationship and communication. Are you interested? I would love to have you there."
4. If you are still scared to ask and can't get over the hump, e-mail the friends you want to ask with the request first, and then follow up personally. You also may want to get together with a few others who want to start a GIG, pray, and then call or go out and invite people right then. That way others can give you the strength and encouragement to invite your friends. The toughest step on this adventure is the invitation. Go for it!

How Do I Lead an Excellent Discussion Time?
1. Lay out some discussion guidelines.
   - ☐ I want you to enjoy yourself.
   - ☐ I want you to listen to each other.
   - ☐ I want you to grow, but I don't care how.
   - ☐ I want you to be curious and to ask questions and express your ideas. Any honest question is appropriate.
   - ☐ I want us to keep going back to the passage together and learning all we can from the wisdom Jesus has for our lives. That can keep us from going on lots of tangents.
2. Bring Bibles and refer to page numbers rather than chapter-verse numbers. (Pre-Christians may have no idea where in the Bible to find the Gospels!)
3. Pay attention to the five stages of a great discussion.
   a. Establish rapport and relevance on the theme of the discussion. For instance, if the study is on how Jesus forgives, ask people to share one thing that's happened in their life that was a little embarrassing. You

could also show a movie clip or play a song that raises a question the discussion will address.

b. Get people into the story, feeling it, imagining it, thinking about it, seeing themselves in it.

c. Help people discuss what is confusing, contradictory or unexpected in the story. Here the energy in the discussion should go up. If it doesn't, heighten the unexpected dimension. For instance, in the story of the prodigal son, help people talk about why the elder son is so ticked off. Often this step happens simultaneously with the previous one.

d. Bring resolution by focusing on the main point of the story and what it shows about Jesus and about our search for meaning, love and belonging.

e. Leave people with a thought-provoking question about their lives. Often this step and the previous one happen together.

Handbook for Groups Investigating God

A new handbook, available through 2100 Productions (608-274-9001), has grown out of the work and experience of people who over the last few years have seen God doing remarkable things through GIGs. People are coming to faith in Christ through the GIGs springing up in communities and on campuses across the country. This handbook contains several essays about the philosophy behind GIGs, as well as multiple resources for training and implementation.

Vision: How could God use your church or ministry in a mighty way in evangelism? The first essay will motivate you and your ministry to put your best effort and energy into reaching people who are not yet in God's family. The lost were Jesus' priority; to share his heart we need to make them ours.

Strategy: Adopting a big audacious evangelism goal for your church or ministry. The second essay challenges you and your ministry to launch as many GIGs for pre-Christians as you have small groups for Christians. Ultimately we want to see a GIG within reach of every person in the country.

Implementation: Developing a GIG strategy for your church or ministry. The third essay explains what it will take to make GIGs a part of everything your ministry does.

Training: Leading a GIG with your friend. This essay offers a practical explanation of the nuts and bolts of a GIG-oriented ministry.

Resources for training. Included in the handbook are a number of training resources to bring your church or ministry to full participation in the GIG strategy. Two passages of Scripture are examined (Acts 8, with discussion questions and teaching notes, and Isaiah 55), and handouts are provided. Participants in your training events will take a spiritual interest survey and be introduced to the bridge diagram and the Circles of Belonging gospel presentation, all of which are provided in the handbook.

Sample studies and resources. This section provides sample GIG studies from various guides, along with information on how to get all the studies from each guide and how to find new studies as they are produced.

Appendix: Are the Gospels reliable? The handbook closes with a helpful essay discussing the reliability of the Gospels.

The handbook is designed to be a complete package for you and your ministry. You should have everything you need as you pray and plan for your ministry's evangelism efforts. I've been awed, along with my colleagues in this project, to watch God reach friends and transform campuses, churches and ministries, making people practically passionate and active for the sake of the gospel. We invite you to join in the adventure!

Appendix 3

GIG STUDIES FROM THE BIOGRAPHIES OF JESUS

THESE STORIES ARE CHOSEN AS A WAY TO HELP PEOPLE WORK THROUGH THE gospel presentation called Circles of Belonging, which appears in chapter thirteen.

At first, all creation was in the circle of belonging.

Study 1: Made for Relationships
Luke 10:25-37

Today we're going to look at what's important in life. Let's start by each sharing something in your life that's important to you. Why is it important, do you think?

Movie clip suggestion: Show the segment in *City Slickers* when Jack Palance tells Billy Crystal that you have to have one thing that is most important and do that one thing. Or you can paint the scene in people's minds if you don't have access to a VCR.

We'll be looking at Jesus and listening to his wisdom, using the biography of Jesus that Luke wrote. Luke was an excellent writer for nonreligious people, and he was a very careful investigative reporter (see Luke 1:1-4).

Now let's get into the story.

Let's look at Luke 10:25-37 on page ____ to get Jesus' wisdom on what that one thing might be. Let's each read a few verses.

First let's look at the interaction between the lawyer and Jesus. What's going on? Why does Jesus answer a question with a question? What's the lawyer after, and what's Jesus after? What does Jesus think is the one thing? How do you respond?

Now let's look at the story Jesus tells.

Just for background, a priest would be like a pastor today, a Levite would be like a real committed churchgoer and leader, and a Samaritan would be like a person from a despised minority who believes in an inferior religion. The Samaritans were from the wrong side of the tracks!

What do you notice about the story? Have you had any bad experiences with religious people? Why do you think it's the despised minority person who adheres to an inferior religion who takes pity and helps? If you were the injured man, how would you feel about the way you were treated by the religious people? the Samaritan? What would you have learned from the experience?

So what do you think is Jesus' main point, in this story and in the first part we looked at?

If you were listening to Jesus at that moment and thinking about your own life, what would you think about? How would you feel? Is Jesus' "one thing" *your* one thing?

We loved other things more than God, resulting in spiritual death.

Study 2: The Good Life
Luke 18:18-30

A well-known beer commercial ends with the line "It doesn't get any better than this." Picture yourself at the end of a day being able to say that. What's happening, or what happened that day so you could say, "It doesn't get any better than this"?

Movie clip suggestion: best day/worst day scene in *City Slickers,* or car singing scene in *Tommy Boy.*

Let's look at Luke 18:18-30 on page ____ and each read a few verses.

For Jesus, eternal life was the good life, the full life, life as it was meant to be lived, both now and forever.

What's the initial question, and how does Jesus' answer help us understand the way he thinks we should live? What do you think of Jesus' answer? Do you think Jesus is just into a bunch of dos and don'ts? Why do you think he disagrees with the man calling him good?

Why does Jesus tell the man to sell everything, give to the poor and follow him? Do you think Jesus demands that of everybody? Why or why not?

Imagine you are you, but just like the man, you go up to Jesus and ask how you can live the good life now and forever. What would Jesus say to you? What might he ask you to give up?

What would the man have gained if he had given up his money and followed Jesus? Notice Jesus' answer to Peter. Does this answer makes any sense to you? Explain.

So what's Jesus' point, and where does that leave you and me?

Jesus died for us, taking on the death we deserve.

Study 3: Finding Love and Belonging
Luke 7:36-50

Think about a group or a clique or an organization you know or are part of. Who is accepted and valued, and who is not? Why?

Alternative question to use if the trust has been growing in a healthy way and you want to go a little deeper: Did you experience a sense of acceptance and belonging growing up in your family or with classmates? Why or why not?

Let's look at Luke 7:36-50 on page ___ and each read a few verses.

Imagine that you are at this dinner party and have been part of the meal celebration. Who is this woman? What does she do, what do you notice, and how do you feel? Can you imagine doing what she did? For information, Jesus would be lying sideways on a sort of recliner chair, facing toward the table and the guests, with his legs going sideways and out.

Pharisees are like the perfectionist, religious, self-righteous people we know. What's this Pharisee thinking, as the host of this party and as a fairly religious, decent kind of person?

What's the comparison Jesus makes, and how does he apply it to the woman and to the host?

So why does this woman act like this? What do you think it is about Jesus that elicits this kind of response?

What do you think Jesus means when he tells her that her sins are forgiven and her faith has saved her?

Are you at all surprised by who feels loved by Jesus and who doesn't? Is that what you expected?

So what is Jesus' point? Which person in the story do you identify with or would want to identify with? Discuss whether you love God like this woman, and whether you *want* to love God as she does.

Movie clip suggestion: You could end by showing the clip from the second part of *Jesus of Nazareth* where Mary comes in and washes Jesus' feet. It is a powerful visual portrayal of this story.

Jesus offers us a way back into the circle of belonging.

Study 4: Coming Home to God
Luke 15:11-32.

Talk about an experience of getting lost. What happened? How did you find your way back home?

Movie clip suggestion: scene in *National Lampoon's Vacation* when the characters get lost in the city and their luggage and hubcaps are stolen.

Jesus talked often about how we can lose our way spiritually. He wanted to help people find their way back to God. So he told this story. Let's read Luke 15:11-24 first.

So tell me what happens here from the point of view of the father. How does he likely feel when the son asks for his inheritance? How does he respond? What does he do while the son is gone, and what does he do when the son returns? How do you think he feels?

Tell me the story from the younger son's point of view. Why do you think the son does what he does? What happens at first, and then later? What does the son do when he hits bottom, and why? Can you share a time you hit bottom or felt pretty down? What happened? What did you do?

What happens when the son returns to the father, and how do you think the son feels at the end? The robe represents the welcome back into the family, the ring represents the father's authority, the sandals represent freedom, and the feast represents celebration and joy. That's how God feels when we come back to him!

What do you think are some of the reasons people decide they want to come back home to God? What keeps people from coming home to God? What might be holding you back?

Let's read Luke 15:25-32, a few verses each.

How does the elder son respond, and why do you think he responds that way? The elder brother is like a lot of religious people who think they already have all the answers but don't have much love for God or enjoyment in life. What does Jesus seem to think of people like that?

So what is God like from Jesus' point of view? Discuss whom you identify with more in your relationship with God: the younger son or the older son. Like the younger son, do you feel you need to come back home to God, and do you want that? Like the older son, do you think you need to learn to celebrate with God and enjoy God's love more, and do you want that?

You can end with "Circles of Belonging" as a summary and ask if they want to meet anymore. Or you can say, "Next week we'll have a party to celebrate our time together, sum it all up and decide if we want to meet anymore."

If you meet on the fifth week, have a party or meal and talk about what people learned in the GIG. Go through the Circles of Belonging gospel message. Ask them where they are and whether they want to meet anymore. Whatever they want, affirm and thank them for the role they have had in your life.

Appendix 4

THE ALPHA COURSE

THE ALPHA COURSE STARTS WITH A BANQUET WITH THE THEME "IS CHRISTIANITY Boring, Untrue and Irrelevant?" At the banquet people are encouraged to attend the Alpha course. The brochure pictured below describes that course and lists the various talks included. At the midpoint of the course, participants attend a seeker retreat focused on the person and work of the Holy Spirit. Often the retreat is a decisive moment at which people commit themselves to Christ. This course has proven to be remarkably effective in bringing people to faith.

What Is Alpha?
Anyone seeking more understanding about the Christian faith can attend the Alpha course. It is designed for nonchurchgoers, but it can also be used as a refresher course for Christians.

Learning and laughter are a key part of the course. A series of fifteen talks tackles key questions at the heart of the Christian faith. These talks can be given by a course leader or presented on video, available from Alpha. It is possible to learn about the Christian faith and have fun at the same time. Laughter and fun help to break down barriers and enable people to relax together.

Pasta and other foods contribute to the welcoming environment. Eating together allows people to get to know each other and develop Christian relationships.

Helping one another is the goal of the Alpha discussion groups. Each person has a chance to participate and contribute as the group discusses the topic, studies the Bible and prays for one another.

Asking anything is allowed. Alpha regards no question as too simple or too hostile. People have a chance to raise their questions and discuss relevant topics together after the talk.

What Happens at Alpha?

The Alpha course extends over eleven weeks, including a celebration supper at the end of the course and a weekend retreat around the sixth week. The course covers a number of topics:

- ☐ Who is Jesus?
- ☐ Why did Jesus die?
- ☐ How can I be sure of my faith?
- ☐ Why and how should I read the Bible?
- ☐ Why and how should I pray?
- ☐ How does God guide us?
- ☐ How can I resist evil?
- ☐ Why and how should I tell others?
- ☐ Does God heal people today?
- ☐ What about the church?

Preparation

The team. Approximately one third of the attenders at each Alpha course should be team members who lead from up front, help in a group or carry out the production tasks of the course (for example, preparing food or setting up chairs). A three-session training course is available on video from Alpha. Two of the sessions (on leading small groups and pastoral care) should take place before the course starts; the third (on ministry) should take place just before the retreat.

The setting. The ideal setting is a home, but if the group outgrows the home, you'll need to find a larger setting with a welcoming atmosphere.

The schedule. The course takes eleven weeks, including the celebration supper at the end. Running three courses each year will maintain the initial momentum. A typical evening may follow this schedule:

6:15—preparation meeting (setup, final instructions and prayer)
7:00—supper (participants eat in small groups)

7:40—worship (optional)

8:00—teaching

8:45—break

9:00—small group discussion (groups of approximately twelve people, with open time for questions and prayer if appropriate)

9:45—end (the ending time should be consistent and known in advance)

The retreat. A typical retreat (see appendix five) may follow this schedule:

☐ Friday

6:30 p.m.—arrive

8:30 p.m.—supper

9:45 p.m.—brief introductory message

☐ Saturday

8:30 a.m.—breakfast

9:30 a.m.—worship and first message

10:45 a.m.—break

11:15 a.m.—second message

12:00 p.m.—small groups

1:00 p.m.—lunch and free time

4:00 p.m.—snacks

5:30 p.m.—worship and third message

7:30 p.m.—supper

9:00 p.m.—group entertainment

☐ Sunday

9:00 a.m.—breakfast

9:45 a.m.—small groups

10:30 a.m.—communion and fourth message

1:00 p.m.—lunch

2:30 p.m.—depart

The celebration supper. At the end of the course a supper party is held to celebrate and share with family and friends about the Alpha course. People should sit with their small groups and introduce their guests. A leader should follow supper with a talk on the relevance of Jesus today, perhaps interviewing one or two people about their experiences with the Alpha course. The leader should announce the dates for the next course and invite people to take part. It may be helpful to hand out a booklet on the relevance of Jesus. (One such booklet, *Why Jesus?* is available through Alpha.)

Materials and information are available with a call to 800-426-6596 or by visiting <www.alphana.org>. Also plan to attend an Alpha training session in a city near you. The program is excellent for developing community that works for pre-Christian people.

Appendix 5

A SAMPLE SEEKER RETREAT
Including an Outline of a Soul Awakening Talk

FOLLOWING ARE OUTLINES OF FOUR TALKS FROM A RECENT SEEKER RETREAT
at which my wife and I were speakers. The flow of the talks is based on the
Circles of Belonging gospel outline in chapter thirteen of this book. The
first talk is a good example of a soul-awakening talk. There is no attempt to
call people to conversion in it. Instead people get good help for their
romantic relationships, and they begin to see that Jesus might have something to do with healing their relational hurts.

The talks also follow the process pre-Christians go through. The first
talk is a *soul awakening* talk. The second includes questions to be discussed
in small groups, helping pre-Christians experience *community*. The third
calls pre-Christians clearly to *conversion*. And the last talk begins them on
the path of *transformation*.

The retreat was called True Love 2000 and was designed as a venue to
which Christians would invite their pre-Christian friends. I hope the talk
titles will stimulate your own creativity as you consider reaching out to
people today.

The talk outlines are followed by some programming suggestions for a
seeker retreat.

Men Are from Mars, Women Are from Venus, and God Is from Somewhere Else

Main point: MaryKay and Rick are really different, but God has helped them stay together.

☐ How they met, didn't like each other, and then fell in love
☐ Conflict and first impressions
☐ Friendship—disco dancing story of melting the ice with each other
☐ Love—how they reluctantly realized they liked each other
  1. Our differences (from John Gray)
☐ In life, he can be Mr. Fix-it, always suggesting how to fix problems, but not necessarily listening very well. She can be the Home Improvement Society, always ready with a long list of things to do and do better!
☐ In conflict, he likes caves and she likes beaches. He likes to withdraw and work it out (go into his cave), she likes to be together as they work it out (like hanging out on the beach).
☐ In commitment, he's a rubber band (one moment falling madly in love, the next moment running for his life) and she's a wave (up and down but always moving in the same general direction toward marriage).
☐ For him, sex leads to feelings of intimacy. For her, sex follows feelings of intimacy.
  2. What holds us together?
☐ Many things, but especially our relationship with God.
☐ Especially, we have learned to forgive by experiencing being forgiven. A story of an experience of hurt and the way God helped us forgive each other.

Roommates, Bad Dates and Soulmates

Main point: Friendship, romance and love are good things, but only God can satisfy us at the center of who we are.

  1. Friendship and roommates: Talk about how good and important friendship is. Then tell of an experience of betrayal and disappointment.

  2. Dating: Acknowledge how wonderful romance is, but then share an experience of hurt and disillusionment when a relationship had become all-important.

  3. Soulmates: Share an experience of love and commitment and oneness, and how good that is. Then show how soulmates can never meet all our needs.

  4. The pattern and consequences of replacing God at the center of our

lives with other things. Include other possible centers: role, achievement, escape, approval. Describe the first two circles of Circles of Belonging.

5. The challenge: What do you tend to put in the center? What are the consequences? Where is God in the circle of your life?

Finding Love and Belonging Through a Relationship with God

Main point: We find love, belonging and identity through inviting God back into the center of our lives.

1. Remind us of the struggle and consequences when other things have replaced God at the center.

☐ MaryKay's testimony

☐ Rick's testimony

2. Draw and explain the Circles of Belonging gospel message, using an overhead projector, a board or PowerPoint.

☐ How can you find love and belonging through a relationship with God?

    a. Admit your other centers and turn from them toward God.

    b. Accept Jesus' life and death for you.

    c. Ask Jesus to come into the center of your life.

☐ Invitation to respond

Invitation into Transformation

Main point: God will help you live a new and transformed life when you've asked him to be at the center.

1. Some of you have asked God into the center of your life this weekend. Others will in the future. Many others have at some time asked God in the past. So how do you experience a changed life? How do you see actual change in the things you want changed—or the things God wants changed?

2. MaryKay's testimony: what helped her life change. Where does she still need change, and how is God still involved?

3. Teach on the "ministry of transformation." End with a prayer for "strengthening of the will" adapted for new believers (see chapter fourteen).

Questions for Small Groups, Following "Roommates, Bad Dates and Soulmates"

1. Think of a good friend, and tell why that relationship has been important to you. What qualities does that person have that you appreciate?

2. Do you think a friendship can become too important? How?

3. What do you like about the whole dating and romance thing, and what don't you like?

4. Could you at all relate to Rick's or MaryKay's stories of rejection?

5. What's really important in your life, and where does God fit in? How has the talk and our discussion stimulated your thinking about what's important to you?

Questions for Small Groups, Following "Finding Love and Belonging Through a Relationship with God"

1. Would you say you believe in God? What are your doubts or struggles?

2. Could you relate at all to Rick's or MaryKay's story of finding God?

3. Where is God in your life: at the center, in the circle somewhere, outside the circle?

4. Where do you want God to be in your life? Outside the circle? Somewhere in your life? At the center of your life? Have you already invited God in, or are you ready to do that now or this weekend? What would keep you from inviting God into the center of your life?

Say a prayer for all the members of your group, briefly, wherever they are in their journey toward God.

Programming Helps for the Seeker Retreat

Talk 1. Use a video clip from *You've Got Mail,* when Ryan and Hanks meet at the party, or when he visits her while she is sick, or from the end of *When Harry Met Sally* when Ryan and Crystal characters get back together. Both movies illustrate communication problems between men and women.

Talk 2. Use "A Real Man" drama. You can get it from Willow Creek at <www.willowcreek.org> or by calling 847-765-5000. Play a contemporary song that elevates a relationship as all-important—try to find a song that is a little extreme!

Talk 3. Use the drama "Only Child" or "Another Day at the Bus Stop," both available at the Service Builder page at the Willow Creek Association website. Or try a video clip from *While You Were Sleeping* where Bullock's character calls off the marriage—during the wedding!

Talk 4. Use the section of Zeffirelli's *Jesus of Nazareth* movie where Mary comes in and washes Jesus' feet with her tears, or where Jesus brings Matthew and Peter together and tells the story of the prodigal son. Both are in part two of that movie.

Appendix 6

CIRCLES OF BELONGING TRAINING SHEET

The Circles of Belonging model for presenting the gospel is reprinted here with instructions for your use. This effective model can be easily memorized and put to immediate use. The left column is the presentation as you would offer it to your friend. The right column is the model with instructions for the presenter. For an example of how the model can be presented, see chapter thirteen.

The Circle of Belonging

At first, all creation was in the circle of belonging.
God made the world. God made you—to love God, to be loved by God. We were made to have God at our center and through God to know we are God's children. With God in the center, we were in right relationship with ourselves and everything else.

Do you long to belong, to know who you are, to know you matter and are deeply and passionately loved by the God who made you? I know I wanted that. So what has happened? Why do we feel so alone, so distant from God?

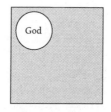

Begin by asking, "Can I share a picture of God's love for us?" Divide the napkin (or whatever you're drawing on) into four quadrants. Draw a circle with God in the center as you share the ideas in the first paragraph. You may want to ask why they think people so seldom feel really connected to God. (Genesis 1:1, Deuteronomy 6:5; Mark 12:29-31)

We loved other things more than God, resulting in spiritual death.

Unfortunately, we choose to substitute something else for God at the center of our lives. Maybe a boyfriend or girlfriend. Maybe a family or cultural background. Maybe achievement or performance. Maybe a role we play. Maybe our sexuality or gender, or approval from our parents or acceptance from our circle of friends. We forget that we are much more than any of these things.

Substituting something else for God at the center of our lives is what the Bible calls sin. And we all sin. We try to run our own lives, we try to create our own identity. We wrap our identity up in these other things, but they can't deliver and they will always disappoint us. Our lives become more fragmented, more painful, more scattered. At the center of our lives, where God should be, we experience an emptiness.

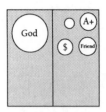

Add the circles representing the things we try to replace God with in the second quadrant. This is a good place to share the things you have replaced God with in your own life. Ask them if they can identify with what you're describing. (Romans 3:23; Ephesians 2:1-2)

I was seeking to wrap my life up in relationships and experiences. If I could only find the right girl, or experience the best high, I would feel better about life. I would discover who I really was. But it wasn't working. I still felt empty and often alone. How are you seeking to fill that emptiness and aloneness? Is it working for you?

In the Bible God tells us that as we reject God in favor of other things, we hurt ourselves, others and God. God hates our choice to replace God with other things. Without God in the center, our identity, our view of ourselves and our relationships with others are distorted. We often feel ashamed of who we are. We end up alone and disconnected. The lack of God at the center of our lives results in spiritual death. If we never turn toward God, that aloneness and emptiness and shame and spiritual death lasts forever! The Bible calls this condition hell.

To me this sounded harsh. Yet it made sense too. I knew I needed something more at the center of who I was. I was starting to want God back in the center. But how could that happen? What could I do?

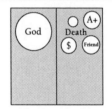

When you talk about the lack of God in the center, write the word *death* over the second quadrant.

Jesus died for us, taking on the death we deserve.
Fortunately, God didn't leave us alone and spiritually
dead. Out of passionate love for us, God wants to be
restored as the center. God wants us to live in our identity as a loved child of God. So God came to us as a
human being, Jesus.

Jesus was God. Jesus created love and acceptance
and belonging wherever he went because God was his
center. He showed people who they really were, and he
showed people how to live with all those other things
in right relationship with the real center.

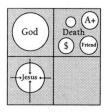

Draw a circle in the third quadrant. Write the name Jesus just
above the center of the circle.
Draw four arrows pointing to
Jesus' name (in the shape of a
cross) to indicate that Jesus
showed people a rightly centered human life. (Mark 15:34;
John 3:16; Romans 5:8)

And then, even though God was his center, he died for
us. He was killed on the cross, taking on all the consequences of our choice to run our own lives and to live
with other things at the center. At the cross Jesus took
on himself the spiritual death we deserved.

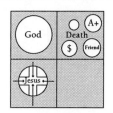

Draw a cross around Jesus'
name.

Jesus offers us a way back into the circle of belonging.
What's more, Jesus didn't just die. He came back from
death, and he is alive today. The evidence that Jesus
rose from death is astonishing. He *is* alive! So he can
live in us, at our center, restoring God to the central
place in our lives. Jesus will forgive us for the pain
we've caused and change us from the inside out. Jesus
can give us the sense of belonging and identity we seek
and restore right relationships with others and the rest
of creation. Because of Jesus we can live in our identity
as God's child, part of God's family.

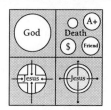

Draw a new circle in the
fourth quadrant. Write Jesus'
name in the center. Emphasize
that Jesus fills the center. Use
arrows to indicate how Jesus
restores our right relationship
with other things in our life.

How does this happen?

☐ We *admit* our false centers and turn from them toward God.

☐ We *accept* Jesus' death for the death we deserve and the hurt we have caused.

☐ We *ask* Jesus to come into the center of our lives, and we *commit* ourselves to him as our forgiver, healer and leader. Through Jesus our real identity—God's beloved child—is reestablished in relationship with God.

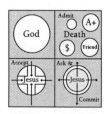

Explain that a commitment to Jesus can change your whole life. This may be a good point to share your commitment story. Ask where God is in the person's life. Ask if he or she would like to know how God could be at the center. Add the words *admit, accept* and *ask* to quadrants two, three and four, respectively; and explain their meaning. Offer to lead a simple prayer to invite God into the center of his or her life. (John 1:12-13; Romans 6:23; 12:9; 1 Timothy 1:16)

Sources Cited

Asimov, Isaac. *Foundation*. New York: Avon, 1951.

Aulén, Gustaf. *Christus Victor*. Translated by A. G. Hebert. New York: Macmillan, 1969.

Cymbala, Jim. *Fresh Wind, Fresh Fire*. Grand Rapids, Mich.: Zondervan, 1997.

Dodd, C. H. *The Apostolic Preaching and Its Development*. Chicago: Willett, Clark, 1937.

Gibbs, Eddie. *ChurchNext: Quantum Changes in How We Do Ministry*. Downers Grove, Ill.: InterVarsity Press, 2000.

Grenz, Stanley J. *A Primer on Postmodernism*. Grand Rapids, Mich.: Eerdmans, 1996.

Hunter, George. "The 'Celtic' Way for Evangelizing Today." *Journal of the Academy for Evangelism in Theological Education* 13 (1997-1998): 15-30.

Jennings, Willie. "Postmodernism and the University." Paper presented at the Emerging Culture Consultation, Downers Grove, Ill., January 2000.

Kotter, John. *Leading Change*. Boston, Mass.: Harvard Business School Press, 1996.

Lawhead, Stephen. *Byzantium*. New York: Harper/Prism, 1996.

Lewis, C. S. *The Weight of Glory and Other Essays*. New York: Macmillan, 1949.

Mittelberg, Mark. *Building a Contagious Church*. Grand Rapids, Mich.: Zondervan, 2000.

Mittelberg, Mark, Lee Strobel and Bill Hybels. *"Becoming a Contagious Christian" Evangelism Course*. Grand Rapids, Mich.: Zondervan, 1995.

Payne, Leanne. *The Healing Presence*. Westchester, Ill.: Crossway, 1989.

Peretti, Frank. *Piercing the Darkness*. Wheaton, Ill.: Crossway, 1989.

Pritchard, Greg. *Willow Creek Seeker Services*. Grand Rapids, Mich.: Baker, 1996.

Stott, John R. W. *Becoming a Christian*. Downers Grove, Ill.: InterVarsity Press, 1950.

Sweet, Leonard. *SoulTsunami*. Grand Rapids, Mich.: Zondervan, 1999.

Tarnas, Richard. *The Passion of the Western Mind*. New York: Ballantine, 1991.

Titanic. Twentieth-Century Fox and Paramount Pictures, Hollywood, Calif., 1998.

Tremayne, Peter. *Absolution by Murder*. New York: Signet, 1997.

Warren, Rick. *The Purpose Driven Church*. Grand Rapids, Mich.: Zondervan, 1995.

Webber, Robert E. *Ancient-Future Faith*. Grand Rapids, Mich.: Baker, 1999.

Willow Creek Association. "Willow Creek Service Builder." <www.willowcreek.org/ServiceBuilder/SB1Home.html>